For Jim Walters

A true believer

With all best,
Michael Frome

Heal the Earth, Heal the Soul

Collected Essays on Wilderness, Politics and the Media

By Michael Frome

Foreword by Ted Williams
Afterword by Dan Small

Published by Bartram Books/Big MPG
811 East Vienna Avenue
Milwaukee 53212
414-332-3900
Fax 414-332-3919
www.BigMPG.com

This book is printed on recycled, acid-free paper.

Manufactured in the United States of America

Cover and book design by Scott Davis

Front and back cover photos by June Eastvold

Library of Congress Cataloging-in-Publication Data
Frome, Michael
Heal the Earth, Heal the Soul: Collected Essays on Wilderness,
Politics and the Media

ISBN-13: 978-0-9790305-0-5
ISBN-10: 1) 0-9790305-0-1

The greatest need of our time is to clean out the enormous mass of mental and emotional rubbish that clutters our minds and makes of all political and social life a mass illness. Without this housecleaning we cannot begin to see. Unless we see we cannot think. The purification must begin with the mass media. How?

Thomas Merton, Confessions of a Guilty Bystander, 1966

He could not and would not prettify the scene. But he dignified it, with a conscientiousness and with standards that were unyielding and with a boundless confidence that if only sound values and solid information could be located in the confusion of events, the citizen reader would distinguish the right from the wrong and uphold the public good.

Editorial in the New York Times January 1, 1977 on the retirement of John B. Oakes as editor of the editorial page.

Books by Michael Frome

Heal the Earth, Heal the Soul

Green Speak: Fifty Years of Environmental Muckraking and Advocacy

Green Ink: An Introduction to Environmental Journalism

Chronicling the West: Thirty Years of Environmental Writing

Regreening the National Parks

Promised Land: Adventures and Encounters in Wild America

Issues in Wilderness Management (editor)

Battle for the Wilderness

The National Forests of America (with Orville L. Freeman)

The Forest Service

Conscience of a Conservationist: Selected Essays

Our Great Treasures: America's National Parks (with David Muench)

The Varmints: Our Unwanted Wildlife

Strangers in High Places: The Story of the Great Smoky Mountains

Whose Woods These Are: The Story of the National Forests

For June Eastvold

Poet, pastor, and healer of earth and soul,

My wife and best buddy

Acknowledgments

Grateful acknowledgment is made to editors of periodicals and books in which these essays and articles first appeared (several with other titles):

"In an Age of Enlightenment wildlife comes first and not last," *Defenders*, 1974; "An Indian hears the whispering of his soul," chapter in *Voices from a Sacred Place: In Defense of Petroglyph National Monument*, 1998; "Haig-Brown's heart was with the working stiffs," *Western American Literature*, 1994; "Panthers wanted – alive, back East where they belong," *Readings in Argument*, Jeanne Fahnestock and Marie Secour, editors, 1985 (excerpted from *Smithsonian*, 1979); "Must our campgrounds be outdoor slums?" *Reader's Digest*, 1969 (*True Magazine*, 1969); "Replacing old illusions with new realities," keynote address, National Association for Interpretation, 1990; "Portrait of a conserver: Horace Albright," *Westways*, 1964; "A man of the parks: Newton B. Drury," *Cosmos Club Bulletin, Living Wilderness*, 1980; "A Kind of Special Breed: Conrad L. Wirth," *American Forests*, 1964; "Amazonia is worth more in its natural state," foreword to *South America's National Parks*, by William C. Leitch, 1990.

"The clock strikes 12 for John P. Saylor," *Field & Stream*, 1974; "Only the individualist succeeds," chapter in *Interpretive Views*, edited by Gary Machlis, 1986; "Regreening the national parks," delivered at commemoration of the seventy-fifth anniversary of the National Park Service, Vail, Colorado, 1991; "A wilderness original: Bob Marshall," foreword to *A Wilderness Original*, by James A. Glover, 1996; "Earth man: Harvey Broome," foreword to *Out under the sky of the Great Smokies*, by Harvey Broome, 2001; "Bitterrooter: Stewart Brandborg," *Wilderness Watch*, 1999; "In wildness is the preservation of the world," delivered at a symposium at Utah State University, 1990; "Afoul of lumber barons and politicians: Charles H. Stoddard," letter to Stoddard family, 1998; "Heal the earth, heal the soul," chapter in *Crossroads: Environmental priorities for the future*, edited by Peter Borelli, 1988.

"Writer with a cause: Richard Neuberger," *Cascadia Times,* 1997; "He dignified the scene: an obit for John Oakes," written for *E-Streeter,* newsletter of *Washington Post* alumni who worked in the old plant, 2001; "Reaffirming the writer's role," *Newsletter* of the American Society of Journalists and Authors, 2000 (also in *American Writer* ("Keeping writing standards high,") 2000; "Illusions of Objectivity," *Montana Journalism Review,* 1999; "Sacred space, sacred power," *International Journal of Wilderness,* 2005.

* * * * * *

I acknowledge further the input and support of the following:

Scott Davis for his creative design of the cover, text and typography; Carl Nilssen of Big MPG for converting the contents from original sources into workable form and later directing printing of the book; Glenn Walters for help in structuring the work into chapter form on my computer; Lisa Friend for indexing and copyediting (as she has done on four of my previous books); Ted Williams and Dan Small for the Foreword and Afterword; Dr. James R. Fazio, of the University of Idaho, for his scholarly counsel, and June Eastvold, my wife, for the photographs on front and back covers and for her encouragement and support.

Contents

Foreword

Objective Advocacy: Lessons from A Legend
By Ted Williams

"He's what all good conservation communicators should be, a gadfly to some, an inspiration to others. You can't, as the old saying goes, make an omelet without breaking some eggs, and our new Chief has cracked more than a few vulnerable shells in his career." – Joel Vance, welcoming Dr. Michael Frome to the Circle of Chiefs, at the Outdoor Writers Association of America, Orono, Maine 1994.

"No writer in America has more persistently argued for the need of a national ethic of environmental stewardship than Michael Frome." – US Senator Gaylord Nelson, of Wisconsin, Washington DC 1974.

"But did he have to name names?" one of the many editors who have fired Mike Frome plaintively intoned to investigators from the American Society of Journalists and Authors. Well, yes he did.

"He gives 'em hell," bragged one of the many editors who have hired Mike Frome. Well, no he doesn't. To borrow the words of Harry Truman, he "just tells the truth on 'em, and they think it's hell."

Frome didn't become a college professor until seven years after I'd finished my schooling, but he is the best writing instructor I've ever had. He started teaching me my sophomore year in college when I read his first conservation column in *Field & Stream*. That was 1967.

Later, during my graduate studies in journalism, my professors pounded home the message that allowing one's opinion to show in an article was as indecent as mooning the dean. Professional writers never pushed, prodded or challenged their readers. They were "objective" in that they presented only "facts." They gave both sides of every story, never hinting that one side might be wrong or which side that might be. They got quotes from both sides, even when one or both sides were lying. They never identified the lies, probably because they didn't recognize them.

It seemed to me that the kind of reporting Frome did was harder and served the reader better. Rather than recycle flack babble and press releases from, say, Weyerhaeuser and the Sierra Club – something readers could get on their own – he dug out the real story. And, while he didn't sermonize, he made it absolutely clear what he thought. How could a writer be so "unprofessional" and work for national magazines?

Frome claims not to have known much about teaching when he entered academia in 1978 as a professor of environmental studies at the University of Vermont. He's wrong because the best writers don't just "report"; they also teach. When Frome got to the classroom he kept doing what he had always done since signing on with the *Washington Post* late in 1945 (after four years in the Army Air Force). He just did it in a different medium.

Frome's central message in print and in class has always been that advocacy journalism is a virtue not a vice, that it's not just okay but essential to have "an agenda," and that if you're an outdoor writer and your agenda is not safeguarding fish, wildlife and the environment, you should be in a different business. Here's how he puts it in his recent book, *Green Ink*, which ought to go out with the directory to all OWAA (Outdoor Writers Association of America) members: "I have heard the command to 'be professional' used in some instances to block expressions of pity, grief, or outrage at wrongdoing.... As practiced by most dailies and other outlets, established journalism continues to suffer under the delusion that objectivity is being maintained. Not only is this a sham, but it does not promote as much digging into contrary views as the alternative advocacy. The best journalism carries authority and a sense of purpose. Literate writing, advocacy writing, contributes to a view of the world that is more rather than less complicated.... Get the facts, but then write them with feeling, your own feeling."

Frome taught me that getting and staying hired is easy. What takes talent, effort and spine is getting fired – or, rather, choosing to get fired when principles are at stake. Frome has done a lot of this, displaying a brand of courage you don't see much in journalism or anywhere. But he also taught me that whenever a door closes behind you another opens ahead.

American Forests has come far since March 4, 1971 when William Towell, then its executive vice president, sent this written order to James Craig, editor of the outfit's magazine, *American Forests*, about its muckraking columnist: "Frome, in the future, is not to write critically about the U.S. Forest Service, the forest industry, the profession or about controversial forestry issues.... I am very pleased, as was the board, that Mike has agreed to this censorship." But Frome had agreed to no such thing. Agreeing would have been easy; getting fired, the path he chose, was not.

Richard Starnes, then Frome's fellow practitioner of advocacy journalism at *Field & Stream*, wrote about the incident in such terse prose that he was able to get the entire story into his title: "How the Clearcutters Tried to Gag Mike Frome."

It still astonishes me that *Field & Stream* and, later, *Western Outdoors* would have hired someone like Frome. He's not a hunter, and he exaggerates with the word "pretty" when he calls himself "a pretty terrible fisherman." I'm even more astonished that he managed to stay at *Field & Stream* seven years, writing 75 conservation columns and a dozen features, always naming names, never pulling a punch. Frome was happy at *Field & Stream*. "Clare Conley (the editor for most of his tenure) gave me free rein, plenty of space and supported me all the way," he says. "I loved writing for the hunters and fishers in the outdoors community and received calls and letters from all over the country with inside information, invitations and pleas to come to investigate issues. I spoke at state wildlife federations, Trout Unlimited chapters and at college and university programs."

I especially liked Frome's "Rate Your Candidate," published before each election. Politicians who got low scores, including Sen. Bob Dole (R-KS) and Rep. Gerald Ford (R-MI), complained bitterly. Sen. John Pastore (D-RI), chairman of the Subcommittee on Communications, which regulated broadcasting, earned only a "marginal" in the 1972 election. In 1974, with Conley gone, *Field & Stream* cancelled "Rate Your Candidate" and fired Frome, explaining that it just didn't like Frome's writing, which may have been true, and later that he was "anti-hunting," which wasn't true. Reporting on the firing, *Time* magazine quoted Conley as saying, "We got vibes from CBS (which owned *Field & Stream* at the time) that they didn't want trouble with Pastore. The word was 'Do what you have to do, but take it easy,'" to which the magazine added: "that Frome refused to do, with the result that he lost his biggest platform."

Even then I respected *Field & Stream*'s right to fire anyone it pleased, but what struck me as much more newsworthy than the firing was the public reaction it generated. Nothing like it has ever been seen in outdoor journalism. Readers picketed CBS headquarters in Washington, DC. Expressing outrage in print were Ray Scott of the Bass Angler Sportsman Society, Jack Lorenz of the Izaak Walton League, Tom Bell of *High Country News*, Fish and wildlife agencies in Massachusetts and Montana, even

Outdoor Life.

On the floor of the U.S. House of Representatives Silvio Conte (R-MA) declared: "Mr. Speaker, I rise to express my dismay and outrage about the censorship and dismissal of Michael Frome, one of the nation's foremost conservation writers... Because he occasionally dared to attack those politicians who control legislation in committees important to CBS, Mike Frome was censored, censured and, finally, dismissed... It is intolerable that CBS, which prides itself as a national symbol and defender of the principles of free speech and free press, can get away with firing Mike Frome because he exercised these principles.... The firing of Mike Frome must be interpreted as a selfish and hypocritical act."

A remarkably accurate prophecy for the next three decades was offered by James M. Shepard, director of the Massachusetts Division of Fisheries and Wildlife, in that agency's magazine, *Massachusetts Wildlife*: "Don't worry about Mike's career. Why should you? He never has. And that, in a nutshell, is why his career has been and will be so illustrious. He's forever getting fired from somewhere, but, to the dismay of those public enemies he publicly probes, he never shuts up." New doors kept opening for him, and they keep opening still.

As a college professor Frome pushed the envelope, too, but it is harder to fire a professor than a writer, and eventually he won the support of most of his colleagues and superiors, liberating them to a degree. The University of Idaho College of Natural Resources now offers the Michael Frome scholarship for excellence in conservation writing. A few ivy-covered deans and department heads he offended in numerous ways (including by bringing me in as a guest lecturer). He challenged and questioned, trained political activists and writers. Believing that people learn by doing, he encouraged his students to get involved and foment change. He sent them into the field to report on real issues, and he had them publish their articles. Sometimes this churned up the locals; but churning is good for everyone save a few tenured conservators of torpor.

Five years ago when I asked Frome to comment about environmental education for an article I was writing for *Audubon* he sent me an excerpt from one of his lectures that gave me an insight into why some in academia view him as a threat: "Education, with only a few exceptions, is about careers, jobs, success in a materialistic world, elitism, rather than caring and sharing; it's about facts and figures, cognitive values, rather than feeling and art derived from the heart and soul; it's about conformity, being safe in a structured society, rather than individualism, the ability to question society and to constructively influence change in direction. A change in direction is critical and imperative. The most important legacy our generation can leave is not a world at war, nor a nation in debt to support a nuclear star-wars system, nor the settlement of outer space, transporting all our worldly problems to the rest of God's universe, nor the breeding of test-tube babies and robotic drones. Our most precious gift to the future, if you will ask me, is a point of view embodied in the protection of wild places that no longer can protect themselves."

I am convinced that the reason Frome has stayed physically young is that he thinks young. He taught me to do the same and, more important, to think for myself and to change my mind when new information came to light. Coming from an ultra-conservative Republican family and deeply involved with sportsmen, wildlife managers and outdoor writers (all of whom tend to be conservative), I had long been instructed to revile "environmental extremists." While the lessons never took, I did distrust some of the people who were said to be "environmental extremists" until I realized that I was one myself, at least by the definition of many of my peers and family members.

In these conservative circles Dave Foreman, a monkey-wrencher in his youth, was and is reviled as the high priest of environmental extremism. And yet, when I sat next to him at a National Audubon Society dinner where he was being honored as one of the "environmental heroes" of the 20th century, I encountered a refined, dignified, intelligent gentleman committed to all the things I am committed to – most of all large-scale habitat protection. Foreman and I both had changed: in different ways and from different directions, but for the better. While I can't speak for Dave, I suspect that, like me, Mike Frome is among the people he can thank for helping him learn to open and change his mind.

And here, from Dave Foreman, is one of the best compliments Mike Frome ever received: "The greatest inspiration you have been to me has not been your knowledge of wilderness issues, but your ability to grow at an age where most people have long since ossified. You're proof that an old dog can learn new tricks. You've been on the cutting edge of conservation since the 1950s. There are damn few people in the world who can make that claim in any field."

My definition of a "legend" is someone who makes a difference, and to make a difference you have to be different yourself. You have to question, probe, and nag. Never can you be content with the status quo. You can't run out of fuel. You can't worry about who you might offend. You punch only with the truth; and, while you never "pull" the truth, you also never bully. Unless you're protecting a source or someone vulnerable to retribution, you need to name names in most cases; but you remember that the people you are naming have feelings, friends and families just like you.

At 86 Mike Frome makes this claim: "I can't do all the things I used to." But I get exhausted just reading about his adventures as he charges around the world with his brilliant and equally energetic wife, June, speaking, writing, hiking, observing, growing. He has written 18 books, and more are on the way. I can't imagine what he used to do that he "can't do" now unless it was bungee jumping.

"Yet," continues Mike, "I cherish the memory of places I've been, things I've done, battles fought whether won or lost, people I've met and worked with. I especially treasure friendships made and kept. I try to keep focused on the pluses in life, believing no matter how bad it gets, we can do something to evoke change, and that we will make it better. The best is yet to come." When Mike Frome tells you that you've got to believe.

(written originally for *Outdoors Unlimited* 2002, updated 2006)

1. In an age of enlightenment wildlife comes first and not last

When Russell E. Train, Administrator of the Environmental Protection Agency, granted authority to spray DDT over 650,000 acres of the Pacific Northwest, presumably to prevent a tussock moth infestation, he relied principally upon scientific and economic data furnished by the Forest Service, an agency committed to commodity production rather than resource protection. Estimates of potential loss, without DDT control, were predicated on commercial timber values only. There was nothing substantive in Mr. Train's equation for the loss of birds, insects and fish, or for the impact on large mammals, or for long-term ecological disruption.

Likewise, when Rogers C. B. Morton, Secretary of the Interior, recently announced receipt of an application from the Alaskan Arctic Pipeline Company for a right-of-way permit across the North Slope, he welcomed it with a declaration that at last the North American Arctic would be unlocked, "its resources made available to meet human needs." Mr. Morton failed to mention, alas, that the Arctic Game Range, the largest, most inviolate wildlife sanctuary on this continent, will be violated. All the pipeline company wants – so they tell us – is to do a little boring for soil samples in surveying the pipeline route. As long experience has painfully demonstrated, the worst step is the first step. For this reason, a similar proposal for test drillings in the Arctic Range was rejected several years ago. This time, however, the Bureau of Sport Fisheries and Wildlife, an agency under Mr. Morton's control, issued the permit without a whimper.

These two happenings tell something about the priorities of modern society. Decisions in questions of land use are determined first and foremost on a basis of commercial values. Ethics, intellectuality, environment and wildlife are secondary. Wildlife comes in last. Every time. Little wonder that Secretary Morton overlooks mentioning the impending disaster hanging over the Arctic Game Range.

Everywhere in the country the land, the rivers, the estuaries and the offshore waters are treated only as commodities to be bought and sold, explored and exploited for material benefits only, never to be safeguarded by one generation as a sacred trust for the next generation to follow. One can find his own examples anywhere. If you examine the proposed superport project within the barrier islands near Port Aransas, Texas, fertile estuarine grass flats and marshes, a nursery and feeding ground for deep-sea fishes, would be destroyed. The Aransas National Wildlife Refuge, home of the whooping crane, and a National Audubon refuge, would be endangered in order to make way for a turning basin, docking facilities, tank farms and related activities. All this to accommodate 250,000-ton tankers, whose spillage would be dumped directly in the bay and estuarine systems.

The same scenario is being written in the Four Corners of the Southwest; Northern Plains of Montana, Wyoming and the Dakotas; Piceance Basin of Colorado, Utah and Wyoming; the Outer Continental Shelves of the Pacific, Gulf and Atlantic. We are being pressed on all fronts by the economic-political power structure to exploit our last slender stocks of natural resources to the point of depletion without restraint. If this process continues, one designated sanctuary after another will fall. No park, refuge or even protected wilderness area will be safe.

The United States has led the way with our super-standards of affluence and waste. At this rate, what can we expect to leave for the next century to use and enjoy? Regardless of how long the remaining resources may last, thoughtful people must challenge whether they should be tapped at all, and ask whether we might be losing something greater for the centuries than gaining for some brief instant of our own time.

We should leave the North American Arctic and other like areas undisturbed in order to fill deep human needs. Kinship with wildlife and plantlife contributes to the humility we need in order to know ourselves as part of the community that is vaster than the community of humankind alone. The earth and its creatures must be loved and respected for their own sake. Otherwise, in due course the whole system of the utilization of resources will break down in collapse.

People who care must demand a reorder of priorities that will demonstrate before the world that ours is an idealist nation not wholly consumed by materialism and corporate greed. Who really runs America? It is time to assert new standards in which growth is not measured in commercial terms alone. Let growth be measured in individual compassion, sensitivity and appreciation of all life forms. Technological overkill of the past several decades has failed. The hour is right for a new age of human restraint and enlightenment.

Defenders of Wildlife, 1974

2. An Indian hears the whispering of his soul

While I was exploring monuments, parks and pueblos in New Mexico in 1996, it occurred to me that just as humans modify places, places influence people, including their views of themselves, of the earth, and of each other. The child who grows up in the out-of-doors will have a world view different from that of the child of the inner-city ghetto. In *The Vanishing American*, Zane Grey's hero, Nophaie, loved most to be alone, "listening to the real sounds of the open and to the whispering of his soul."

As Mary Austin wrote in *The Land of Little Rain*, "For all the toll the desert takes of a man, it gives compensations, deep breaths, deep sleep, and the communion of the stars.... Go as far as you dare in the heart of a lonely land, you cannot go so far that life and death are not before you."

Trouble is, there's not much left of the lonely land. Places have changed, and people with them. I remember once, more than forty years ago, driving cross-country with three friends. Heading west beyond Cheyenne, Wyoming, we ran out of gas. The very first fellow to come by stopped to help. Then he drove forty miles to the nearest town and returned with a can full of gas that he insisted on paying for. That doesn't happen much anymore, in an increasingly crowded world, where cities and suburbs and freeways and malls look alike and could be anywhere, and good people are strangers instead of neighbors.

Thankfully, we have our national parks and national monuments to serve as sanctuaries, sacred space, reminders of the original America, always uplifting and inspiring: I feel we need them now more than ever, while moving through stressful, disorienting times. And when I came to Petroglyph National Monument, where I plainly heard "the whispering of the soul" and joined "the communion of the stars," I thought here now is a model of respect for the earth and for each other, affording civilization a new and better way to address spiritual and community needs in the twenty-first century.

Petroglyph National Monument, with its eloquent ageless images, is a national treasure of transcendent value and meaning, no less than Yellowstone, Yosemite or the Grand Canyon. So it saddened me while in Albuquerque to read a statement attributed to the Monument superintendent, Judith Cordova: "You can't please everyone. We are not a rural area. We are an urban area." That did not ring true, coming from the guardian of such a choice living cathedral.

Consequently, on returning home, I wrote for clarification to John Cook, the Southwest regional director of the National Park Service. I hoped he would agree that personnel of his agency are not mandated to please everyone, but to do their best to protect the treasures in their trust. It grieved me when the letter I received from Mr. Cook reiterated the same old political pap about "conflicting public ideas" and "appropriate balance" between preservation and use.

No, Petroglyph National Monument should not be administered as an urban area for recreationists on bikes and horses, nor "balanced appropriately" with a six-lane highway. To the contrary, the Monument should be nurtured and enhanced as a sacred site, or a comprehensive complex of sacred sites. The real challenge as I see it is not whether to build the proposed road, nor what kind of recreation to foster at the Monument but how to look at the landscape with a point of view that rises above the ordinary into the higher order of ethics and spirituality.

That is what national parks are meant to help us do. National parks, monuments and historic shrines constitute a gallery of America and Americana at their best. True, virtually everywhere these precious places are overused, misused, polluted, inadequately protected, and unmercifully exploited commercially and politically. Clearly, we need to redefine and reassert the rightful role of national parks in the fabric of contemporary society.

And so too the role of the Native American experience and the lessons it embodies for all. Consequent to destroying most of traditional culture, chronic welfare, illness, unemployment, alcoholism and addictions have become an everyday part of Native American life. Yet there is much from which to draw that is enriching and elevating, that engenders love of home, as a particular place, and love of inner self as well.

I observe Native Americans, for all their travails, still honoring the earth and life as divine gifts. On the Northwest Coast where I live, native peoples cherish the giant cedar, hemlock, and Douglas-fir of the cold rain forest, not simply for canoes and longhouses, but as sources of a sacred state of mind where magic and beauty are everywhere. They want to be part of a modern world, while kindling and rekindling earth-based tradition and culture.

The American West has forever been a magic part of the universe, rich in diverse miracles of nature. Long before the advent of civilization as we know it, humans paid homage to these wonders and considered them sacred – the mesas, canyons, badlands and grasslands, deserts, geysers and glaciers, snow-covered volcanic domes, rushing rivers, surf-pounded rocky coast and massive mountains of rock that form the backbone of the continent, thousand-year-old redwood forests, and even older bristlecone pines, growing in their separate environments where other trees cannot make it.

Now is the hour in history for those who hope to heal the earth to join with those who hope to heal the souls to bring something new to bear. Compassion and caring must be at the root of values to make them valuable. Compassion belongs at the root of conservation, embracing a concept of freedom, human dignity and the American spirit, recognition that we are all connected, as brothers and sisters of common origin, common destiny.

Sacred space, with sacred power, is at the heart of a moral world governed by peace and love, a way of life with a spiritual ecological dimension. To say it another way, democracy is what we make of it, a system under which we the people get what we deserve and what we demand. In this age of distrust and disillusionment, answers come when intangible values of the human heart take precedence above an entrenched system in which a small minority controls wealth and power.

Human touch, not money, is required. In Memphis, Tennessee, the Citizens to Preserve Overton Park during the 1960s and 70s were determined to save one of the finest urban forests in the world from proposed construction of a highway through the middle of it. They were forced to contest merchants, developers and public officials, but also the two powerful Memphis daily newspapers. Nevertheless, the citizens group insisted that an established park represents an integral and sacred part of the American city, that it makes the city habitable, and that it would make more sense to locate the highway elsewhere or not build it at all.

The Overton Park case, because it involved federal highway funds, was debated in Congress and before the Supreme Court. It was tough going. The citizens felt that even though the park might be lost, their lives were enriched for each day they saved it. Ultimately, Overton was spared, and it still enhances the landscape and quality of life of Memphis. Thus, it strikes me that as long as the petroglyphs remain intact, they will contribute immeasurably to the character of Albuquerque and will be a source of pride and hope to Americans everywhere.

from *Voices From a Sacred Place: In Defense of Petroglyph National Monument*, 1998.

3. Haig-Brown's heart was with the working stiffs

> There was rhythm to Slim's fishing: the reaching cast, two steps downstream, the long arc of the searching fly, the careful holding at the end, recovery of line and the new cast. Slim broke the rhythm without destroying it, sometimes shortening line to cover a sunken rock, sometimes reaching farther out, perhaps flopping the forming belly of the line upstream to delay the pull of the current, occasionally stripping line from the reel after the cast to let the fly carry down in its line for a few feet more. And when the fish took, there was no haste or anxiety in his response. He expected every move, every sharp turn and run and leap, controlling each one as it came with light easy movements of hand and body.

I would expect that kind of word picture from Roderick Haig-Brown. Nearly thirty years after his passing, he is still the fly fisherman's fly fisherman, the apostle of grace on the stream, of being there, in human harmony with the setting, as an attainment in itself. For such is the essence of most of his twenty-eight books, which even now inspire good feeling, with humility, about God's outdoors.

But this book, *Timber*, first published in 1942 and now reprinted by Oregon State University Press – one of only two novels by Haig-Brown – is more about Slim himself than about his fishing, and about Slim's bosom companion, Johnny, and their fellow loggers, and about life in the woods. And about death, the chronic sacrifice of working people to the work they do, by choice as well as need.

Haig-Brown wrote about the culture of the Pacific Coast loggers from his own experience; he was an insider. When he first came to America from England as an eighteen-year-old, he earned his living in the woods of western Washington. Then he moved north to British Columbia, specifically to the Campbell River country of Vancouver Island, where he pursued his writing career amid some of the last great forests in North America – much the same forests that now, in our time, are under intense attack.

In his introduction, Glen A. Love, a professor of English at the University of Oregon, suggests the heritage of cut-and-run logging is the realization that "we are less noble than that which we have destroyed." As evidence, he cites another Haig-Brown work, *Above Tide:*

> It is in the history of civilizations that conservationists are always defeated, boomers always win, and the civilizations always die. I think there has never been, in any state, a conservationist government, because there has never yet been a people with sufficient humility to take conservation seriously.

Maybe so, but the loggers depicted in *Timber* were pretty noble people, which for me kindles more hope than despair. Haig-Brown's timbermen could be tender at times, and they could be tough. They were loyal to their own kind. After Big Al, a card shark as crooked as a dog's hind leg, made off with Old John's paychecks for five months, young Johnny tracked down the gambler, bashed him with both fists and recovered everything. Another time, after their friends, Scotty and Don Henty, were tricked by pimps and rolled in a fancy-house of prostitution in Vancouver, Slim and Johnny went down from the logging camp and cleaned the place out.

Haig-Brown clearly was bent on the mission of showing the upside and downside of loggers' lives. He may not have been a revolutionary, but his heart was all with the working stiffs on the ground, creating wealth for absentee owners. When Slim spoke strongly for going union on the job, Johnny's wife, Julie, said he was thinking only of himself. To which Slim replied:

"I'm thinking of me and Eric and old Tom and Johnny and every other slave that drags logs out of the bush till he's too old or too crippled or they make up their minds to blacklist him."

In due course both Slim and Johnny were fired and blacklisted. They were tops in their trade, but forced to work where they could, for a small time, cost-cutting outfit. A tree – one that was "conky" and never should have been rigged – broke in the logging process and death claimed another victim.

As a novelist, Haig-Brown was not a powerhouse, and as a novel *Timber* is not exactly memorable. However, I'm glad OSU Press has included the book in its Northwest Reprints series, for it is memorable as a Haig-Brown souvenir and as a period picture of life in the old logging camps. The author knew the men, their equipment, their distinctive logging lingo, and their women, who stuck by them come what may.

Reading *Timber* recalls a visit I made more than thirty years ago to one of the last of the Northwest logging camps. Most men working in the woods had already shifted to town living but the Simpson company still operated Camp Grisdale, on the Olympic Peninsula. In the evening we responded to the "guthammer," the dinner bell. The men with whom I ate were well mannered.

The cookhouse, laid out like a cafeteria with long benches, was immaculate. Why should this be so? I asked the "gut robber" (the head cook). "Well, in a logging camp," said the old gentleman, "cooks are proud because they know their customers."

After supper, we sat and talked. The loggers recalled the old days. Conditions were rough. Talking was not allowed at meals. There were shacks for bunkhouses. You packed your own bedroll and blankets. You worked as long as it was light enough to work. Logging was hazardous and it was not considered unusual when a man was killed in the rigging – that was Haig-Brown's point.

How, or why, I asked, did conditions change? Was it enlightened corporate interest? Government intervention, as in the New Deal?

"Politicians, hell!" one man replied. "It was the union. The union changed conditions." So old Slim was right, after all.

But perhaps the larger question I should ask now, as the great Northwest forests go down, is whether society can ever find peace, healing and reconciliation within itself. Or must the last tree follow the last whale and then, as Melville wrote, the last man smoke his last pipe, and then himself evaporate in the last puff? I, for one, prefer to foresee the best, taking hope and heart from Emerson's optimism and his belief that the human soul is capable of transcending the physical and material to achieve redemption. That is what Roderick Haig-Brown's work and way of life were all about.

From *Western American Literature*, 1994

4. Panthers wanted – alive, back East where they belong

The following article on panthers is unique among the CP [categorical proposition] arguments in this section because it argues not about what a thing is, but whether it is. What we have here is an existence argument claiming that there is evidence that the eastern mountain lion has survived. The author, Michael Frome, is a self-proclaimed aficionado of the Smoky Mountains who has written a book on them, *Strangers in High Places*. Frome is no sensationalist asserting that he has sighted marvels; he is careful to qualify his claims and assess his evidence, though his convictions and his attitude about the survival of the mountain lion come through.

"Panthers Wanted" first appeared in the *Smithsonian*, a wide-circulation magazine published by the Smithsonian Institution in Washington, whose readers tend to be more urban than rural. As you read this essay, think what you would have to do to convince people that you had seen a creature no one believes in.

On a July evening in 1975, five Great Smoky Mountains National Park maintenance workers were lounging on their bunkhouse porch watching a doe and two yearlings. Suddenly the deer fled into the forest and a large, grayish cat with a long tail emerged from the woods and bounded after them. The five men followed quickly, but found nothing more than tracks along a creek. They were convinced, however, that they had seen a panther hunting its traditional prey.

The report they filed in late September 1975 triggered a new sense of awareness of the largest, rarest and most secretive of the wild American cats. The Eastern panther was thought long ago to have followed the trail into oblivion of the great auk, Labrador duck, heath hen, passenger pigeon and sea mink. Recent sightings by some professional biologists, wildlife personnel, and forest and park rangers show this may not be the case. The Eastern panther may be coming back from the brink of extinction for a second chance.

For me the news was especially exciting. For years I've been an aficionado of the Great Smokies, the half-million-acre mountain sanctuary astride the North Carolina-Tennessee border. More than fifteen years ago I had asked the then park naturalist about reintroducing the panther into the Smokies. After all, national parks are supposed to be wildlife sanctuaries and I can't think of any better suited for such a role than the Great Smoky Mountains. Fifty years ago, or less, it was not uncommon for mountaineers to catch sight of the sleek panther (or "painter" in the vernacular) three or four times a year, or to hear its shrill song pierce the wilderness night, and the animal's hams and shoulders were the source of "painter bacon." Even now Panther Creek, Panther Mountain, Cat Run, Painter Branch and Painter Creek are familiar place names in the Smokies and neighboring Nantahalas across the Little Tennessee River.

The biologist to whom I had posed the question responded flatly that the big cat requires too much room even to be considered for reintroduction, and that its day in these mountains was definitely done.

Now we know better. "It appears that nature has succeeded where the National Park Service feared to tread," Boyd Evison, who was the park superintendent (and who has personally seen panther tracks), conceded quite willingly when I was last in the park. "There seems no reasonable doubt that there are cougars in the park; and it seems likely that they have been here for some time. Very little seems to be known about their habits and needs in this kind of country, but the park, if kept free of excessive development, offers the best sanctuary for cougars north of the Everglades and east of the Rockies."

The 1975 observation in the park and concurrent reports of panthers along the Blue Ridge Parkway in North Carolina stimulated me to investigate the whereabouts of the big cat, one of the least known of North American mammals today, not only in the Southern mountains but throughout its range. I found these lonely wanderers of our mountains and forests far more widespread than I could possibly have dreamed. The numbers of animals must be dangerously low, but they apparently are breeding and the long thread of life, though tenuous, remains unbroken.

Felis concolor, "cat all of the same color," varies from light brown or gray to soft reddish brown, or tawny, possibly changing with the season. In the United States and Canada there are fifteen subspecies, all essentially the same animal. Many names have been given, including catamount (for cat of the mountain) in the Northeast, cougar in Canada, panther in the Southeast, mountain lion in the West, "el leon" in the Southwest (to contrast with "el tigre," the jaguar), puma in South America, as well as red tiger, silver lion, mountain devil, mountain screamer, deer killer and king cat. Now it is known mostly as panther, puma, cougar, mountain lion or long-tail cat.

That unmistakable tail is as long as an African lion's, though the panther is only half the size of the king of cats. The average male weighs about 150 pounds, the female about 100, though a large animal may weigh 200 pounds and measure eight feet in length. Our American lion is lean and lithe, endowed with tough skin, sharp claws and sharp teeth.

Though panthers are expert hunters, worthy of a sportsman's admiration, sport hunters long despised them as competitors for deer and played a key role in doing them in. "For the sake of deer supply," argued *Forest and Stream Magazine* in 1885, "the panthers should be systematically pursued and destroyed, and the bounty should be such to encourage this." Likewise, when the nation's leading sportsman, Theodore Roosevelt, became President, he denounced the panther as "a big horse-killing cat, the destroyer of the deer, the lord of stealthy murder, facing his doom with a heart both craven and cruel."

Though deer are the main prey, a panther will eat almost anything. It does humans a good turn by devouring rabbits and rodents, but earns the wrath of stockmen by taking an occasional sheep or calf. Its diet includes porcupine, fox, skunk, badger, frogs, slugs, grasshoppers and even its little cousin, the wildcat.

In the late 1940s a Canadian biologist, Dr. Bruce S. Wright, equated the relationship between panther and deer and came up with a surprisingly hopeful forecast. Wright had observed new forests and abandoned farms developing into first-class deer habitat and hunters encouraging the increase in deer. He predicted that panthers would follow the deer back into new habitats in the East.

The Eastern panther in 1972, according to Wright, had passed the immediate danger of extinction, but only by "the merest fraction." He estimated the total number surviving in eastern North America, exclusive of Florida, at not more than 100 (with the largest number, 25 to 50, in New Brunswick) and possibly fewer, yet he foresaw the animal making a slow comeback in both the Southeast and North, from Florida to the

Laurentians, providing it was given protection.

Despite reports of sightings up and down the Eastern seaboard during the 1960s, many government agencies and scientists remained dubious. Reports of panthers often turned out to be cats, dogs or spooks in the night. Even today some biologists concede only that the panther may exist and refuse to grant anything further in the absence of an acceptable photograph of the animal in the wild, a freshly killed specimen or a confirmed sighting by a scientifically trained observer. Ten years ago the official view of the National Park Service was simply stated: "There are no panthers in the Great Smoky Mountains." Anyone suggesting otherwise was subject to ridicule. Pranksters made things worse here and there by dropping the remains of a panther that had died in captivity, or by creating a trail with a dismembered limb. One or two footprints may be faked realistically, but not a whole trail complete with natural signs, and a competent tracker can spot a fraud in a short time. But the pranks made the whole idea of living panthers seem like a fraud or joke.

Until recently, seeing one was a little like seeing the Loch Ness monster, a vision best kept to oneself. But not any longer. Reports of sightings are solicited rather than ridiculed. And instead of being a despised predator, the panther is increasingly viewed as a prized species that must be rescued from extinction.

Field biologist Robert L. Downing has begun a five-year project, funded jointly by the Forest Service and Fish and Wildlife Service, to search for panthers and panther signs in the Southern mountains. From his headquarters at Clemson University, South Carolina, Downing has established a network of contacts among state and federal resource agencies to help screen, and validate, sighting reports.

One of the first submitted to him, a photograph of a panther track, came from West Virginia early this year. "It's the first I've seen personally and I'm pretty positive it's authentic," he told me.

The three national park units in the Appalachians – Great Smokies, Shenandoah and the Blue Ridge Parkway – are cooperating with Downing in the search for cats, tracks and scats. A young Virginia outdoorsman and expert tracker, Champlin Carney, has been hired to search Shenandoah for tracks and to attempt to obtain photographs using a self-tripping camera.

So goes the search in southern Appalachia, but it's not the only area of interest and activity. New Hampshire officials are cautious believers:

"Although none has been authenticated, enough sightings have been reported by people of good judgment that our department now considers there is a distinct possibility that the mountain lion is making a comeback in our state," says a spokesman for the New Hampshire department of game management.

Reports have been made continually in Massachusetts. West Virginia has stronger evidence. In April 1976 a young 100-pound male was shot by a farmer near Droop Mountain State Park after he saw it attacking his sheep. Though several sightings have been reported in the rugged high forests of Pocahontas County, this was believed to be the first panther killed in West Virginia in at least 50 years. One week later a second mountain lion was located on another Pocahontas County farm. The cats may have been wild or released by someone; yet sightings in relatively undeveloped areas, particularly in national forests, argue against the oft-expressed idea that all such animals must be "escapees from captivity." Besides, there aren't that many zoos or keepers of pet panthers in the Appalachians.

Blue Ridge Parkway rangers reported seeing a mother panther and two cubs near the Pisgah campground on at least two occasions as recently as 1977, a single panther near Frying Pan Tower Lookout, one of the wildest sections of the Blue Ridge, and another single panther at Gales Mine Falls, at the edge of the Asheville watershed.

In the Great Smokies, Ray DeHart, a retired trails foreman of the national park, within the past five years has seen three panthers on hiking trails – including one chasing a wild boar along the Appalachian Trail.

Lions clearly have learned to avoid men. They are shy but inquisitive about humans and sometimes like to be around them, sometimes seen, sometimes unseen, like phantoms. The panther seems to be a puzzling combination of what humans call courage and cowardice. Smaller cousins, the wildcat and lynx, are much more ferocious when cornered or trapped. The panther might attack a bear one day and run from a small dog the next. Complaints of depredation are surprisingly few, and so are unprovoked attacks.

At present the Eastern panther either survives, or may possibly survive, in south central Canada and northern Maine, the White Mountains, isolated areas in Massachusetts, the Adirondacks, the Appalachian Mountains from western Pennsylvania down through Alabama, lowlands of South Carolina and Georgia, southern and central Florida, hardwood bottomlands of northern Louisiana, and the Ozarks of southern Missouri, Arkansas and eastern Oklahoma.

Firm, conclusive data are very difficult to come by. The Eastern panther has been photographed alive only in Florida, with one possible exception. While tramping in the Adirondacks in 1972, Alex McKay, a New Yorker, saw a huge cat stalking silently about 20 feet ahead of him. The cat, seeming to sense him simultaneously, crouched low in the grass and stared with yellow-almond eyes. McKay raised his camera, snapped the shutter and looked down briefly to wind the film. When he looked up again the big cat had vanished.

The single picture he had taken revealed only a feline head with dark cheek patches, a clear muzzle, those glaring almond eyes, and the faint outline of the body crouched in the grass. The State Museum in Albany advised him that a photo is not acceptable documentary evidence; only the fresh skin of a specimen could be considered authentication of the animal's occurrence – yet it's against the law to collect the skin of an endangered species…

Many biologists and wildlife officials shun discussion of the Eastern panther. They seem to fear that recognizing the animal's existence would encourage hunting, regardless of its status as an endangered and protected species. They could be right. "The greatest danger to the panthers today," wrote Bruce Wright, "is from the 'shoot it to prove I saw it' philosophy." And Aldo Leopold's first response thirty years ago on learning that panthers survived in New Brunswick was: "We must not tell anybody."

In a recent study undertaken for the United States Forest Service, biologist George Lowman urged complete protection as "the most necessary step" for management of the panther in the East.

National forests in the White Mountains, Green Mountains, Southern Appalachians, Florida and the Ozarks are all designed to serve many purposes, including wildlife preservation. In places, national forests border national parks, including Shenandoah, the Blue Ridge Parkway and Great Smoky Mountains, and are like extensions of them.

"As much of each national forest as possible should be maintained in unbroken undisturbed tracts," urged Dr. Lowman. "Certainly any type of habitat reduction should be avoided."

Among the states, North Carolina has moved with particular zeal. In

1971 it granted complete protection. Two years later Dr. Frederick S. Barkalow Jr., Professor of Zoology at North Carolina State University, began to solicit photographs or casts of tracks. Most recently the North Carolina State Museum of Natural History issued 1,000 posters ... as part of the first statewide effort to obtain reports.

With passage of the Endangered Species Act of 1973, federal agencies are obligated to give priority to saving the panther and its habitat. The Blue Ridge Parkway and Great Smokies National Park top the list because evidence of the panthers' presence there is so strong.

As Boyd Evison, who is now Assistant Director of Operations for the National Park Service, puts it: "The cats' only real enemy is Man and we will do what we can both to prevent poaching and minimize 'people activities.' You and I may not see one of these lions, but knowing they are there means a lot to us."

* * * * * *

QUESTIONS FOR DISCUSSION

1. The thesis of this article is not difficult to find. But why is it so carefully qualified with a "maybe"? Why doesn't the author just boldly proclaim that the eastern mountain lion exists?

2. What attitude toward the preservation of panthers does the article assume on the part of its audience? Can you imagine an audience that would not share that attitude?

3. How many different kinds of signs did the author collect? What kind of evidence would convince a skeptical biologist that the animal had returned to its original habitat? Can you order the signs according to their reliability? What makes some signs less reliable than others?

4. Why was the photograph of a large cat taken in the Adirondacks not accepted as documentary evidence by the state museums in Albany, New York?

5. What kind of evidence would be required to convince doubters that not just isolated escapees from zoos but a good number of the species *felis concolor* had reestablished itself? Would the evidence have to be different in kind or amount?

6. This article gives a great deal of background information, which is nevertheless relevant to the argument. How do accounts of the panther's

prevalence in the past (as evidenced in place names) and the clear definition of the panther's characteristics work in the argument?

7. Imagine how difficult this existence argument would be without a clear definition of *felis concolor* obtained from earlier times and other habitats. How would interpreters otherwise know what the evidence was supposed to represent? Is the absence of definition the problem with arguments for the existence of the Loch Ness Monster, Bigfoot, and the Chesapeake Bay Monster?

From *Readings in Argument*, Jeanne Fahnestock and
Marie Secor, editors, 1985.

5. Must our campgrounds be outdoor slums?

A funny thing happened in an Iowa state park last year. The place was full of campers, all "roughing it" in search of surcease from city ways. The trouble was, they plugged in so many coffeepots, television sets, electric guitars, razors, overhead lights and portable refrigerators that they blew out the park transformer!

The episode typifies much of the outdoors scene today. Wherever you travel in America, you're sure to see flotillas of trailers and camper vans congested in their special parking lots – treeless, transplanted suburbias that utterly insulate the camper from the environment. Many beautiful forest settings and lakeshores have been degraded into chaotic, blighted camps, with cars jammed hubcap-to-hubcap and tent dwellers living peg-to-peg.

The slum conditions vary only in degree and form, ranging from over-use and overcrowding to litter, defacement, stream pollution, vandalism and crime (serious crimes in the national parks have increased by 138 percent in the last three years). For instance, at the beginning of the winter of 1967-68, the 320 campsites at Everglades National Park, Florida's pre-eminent natural area, were loaded to more than twice their capacity. Campers were often awakened in the middle of the night by strangers desperate for a place to camp and pre-empting half of already occupied campsites. Once this was tolerated, everything went downhill. Toilets were overcrowded; garbage was thrown everywhere.

Blighted campgrounds are also prevalent in many areas of New England, where some state administrations are not as progressive as they should be in furnishing public facilities. Of 1850 campsites in Connecticut, virtually half are crowded into one park, Hammonasset Beach. Until this year in most state-park sites, Connecticut residents were permitted to camp for the entire season. Consequently, Hammonasset, with two miles of beach front, became absolutely mobbed on weekends, the tents flapping in a planless open field, many with strange semi-permanent additions that had to be seen to be believed.

Even the glorious wilderness areas of the West have been afflicted. The foremost camping slum in America during the 1960's has been Yosemite Valley, jewel of California's Yosemite National Park. The problems began when the narrow valley, seven miles long and less than a mile wide, was overrun with summer campers, and the Park Service hewed to its traditional policy of trying to accommodate them all. Traffic became bumper-to-bumper, and the campgrounds degenerated into tent-city tenements. By the mid-60's the summer population of the valley had risen to urban levels – 40,000 to 50,000 on weekends – and so had booze consumption and the crime rate. The heart of a great park had become the Coney Island of the West.

Because of such depredations, arguments blaming modern campers – "They don't give a damn about nature; they're just a bunch of slobs who destroy everything they touch" – have multiplied. But a study of Yosemite and other natural sites shows that these charges aren't true. The root cause of camping blight is congestion. A lake may be rich in appeal when ten people are on its shores, and it may retain most of that appeal with fifty, or even 250. But at some point, sheer numbers alone must transform a pleasant campground into a slum. Private campgrounds are no better. Donald A. Williams, recently retired Administrator of the Soil Conservation Service, an agency of the Department of Agriculture, wrote last autumn, "Camping areas can quickly deteriorate if those in charge lack the willingness to forgo extra income by putting up the 'No Vacancy' sign when no vacancies exist." The farmer living next to a popular national park or forest often knows little about facility design or camping itself; he's likely to pick an abandoned cow pasture, regardless of drainage, put up a sign and an outhouse, and call it a campground. The unhygienic congestion may contribute to stream pollution, soil erosion and flooding. Yet he is rarely reprimanded by county or state agencies.

Despite the many things wrong, some encouraging steps are being taken. In Everglades Park, then-superintendent Roger Allin, for instance, began in the middle of the 1967-68 winter season to manage the campgrounds for optimum benefit. The number of campers was strictly limited to available sites, and the improvement was immediate. In 1966, the National Park Service began to clean things up in Yosemite. NPS Director George B. Hartzog, Jr., ruled that if the natural valley was to survive, it must be operated within its capacity. Camping areas were clearly defined, and rangers now assign campsites to parties when they arrive. When the valley campgrounds are full, visitors are dispatched to other areas in the park. By limiting the number of parties to sites available, the throng of campers was cut in half. But those who get in are treated to better park values. Furthermore, restricting camping on the valley floor to seven days (or to fourteen days elsewhere in Yosemite) has enabled more people each year to enjoy the experience.

Many private campgrounds are following the same principles. Kampgrounds of America (KOA), a franchise operation, generally furnishes safe, sanitary quarters. The growth of the National Campground Owners Association is bringing a much-needed sense of professionalism to its members. The Family Camping Federation has started to inspect and accredit campgrounds.

Where public officials and politicians combine vision and courage, camping slums do not exist. New Hampshire is a case in point. The state has no fewer than 10,000 campsites in 125 areas of all kinds, from public wilderness to highly developed private facilities. One of the newest units in the system is Pawtuckaway State Park, distinguished by its well-spaced sites, one of the first requisites of the non-slum campground.

"Within one hour after this park was opened in 1966, it was full," Russell Tobey, director of state parks said. "We've learned that we must close campgrounds once all the sites are occupied. A few years ago, we thought we were doing the kindly thing to make room for everybody. But we suffered dire consequences in overcrowding and in overstrained staffs, roads and water systems. We concluded that we must strive for optimum, rather than maximum, development. Furthermore, this policy has encouraged private campgrounds all over the state. They now number more than a hundred, and are a considerable factor in the state's economy."

Vermont pioneered a system of state-park camping reservations that a few other states have adopted. Ideally, this will become the policy in many more state and federal areas. Ohio, in the midst of a six-year, $100-million improvement program to create thousands of campsites in existing and new state parks, provides three classes of campgrounds: Class A, with electricity, flush toilets, laundry and showers; Class B, with simple facilities, well water and secluded wooded sites; and Primitive, with pit-type latrines, waste containers and not much more. California's excellent parks also have types A, B and C to meet varying tastes, and last year the state instituted a reservations system with much success. Now the Forest Service is building its new campgrounds on a scale of six different types, to provide for a broad spectrum of "recreation experience levels" from high-density development to wilderness areas.

All of these improvements are good, but not good enough. A national camping program is required. It must perceive what the camping boom is all about – the fact that there is a powerful longing in mankind to return to nature. And since most campers come to the woods with only the foggiest notion of what the wilderness is all about, it must provide more education for our urban population in the care and use of the natural environment.

One proposal worth considering would be to divert all trailers to private campgrounds outside the parks. Trailers are increasingly difficult to accommodate on the campgrounds and parking areas; they require as much space as buses, yet carry only a handful of people, and a trailer is closer in spirit to a motel on wheels than to the kind of natural experience for which national parks are fundamentally designed.

At present, lack of money is the big stumbling block in the way of camping reforms on a national scale. Operating under niggardly appropriations from Congress, the staffs of national parks and forests cannot maintain properly their old areas, let alone develop new ones. Personnel ceilings have already been rolled back to 1966 levels, which means fewer rangers to protect more people. If federal agencies cannot be adequately funded to provide for the safety of the American people, then we should insist that they cut back their operations. This concession to reality would assure quality camping at whatever areas can remain open. And such a schedule should continue in force until Congress agrees to furnish enough money for these public programs.

The ultimate decision is up to the public. Camping is a healthful use of leisure time, a means of release for millions who live in the sardine can of modern urban society. They deserve the best and should insist upon it. When they do, camping slums will no longer exist.

From *Readers's Digest,* 1969.

6. *Replacing old illusions with new realities*

I was privileged in November 1990 to keynote the annual convention of the National Association for Interpretation at Charleston, South Carolina. These were mostly people who used to be called "naturalists" but now "interpreters" for their work in national parks, state parks and nature centers. At the outset I explained that I was able to relate to the theme of the meeting, "The Past is Prologue – Our Legacy, Our Future," having recently completed the manuscript of a new book, *Regreening the National Parks*. Most of the book, as I explained at the outset, treated history as the essential foundation for previewing the national parks of tomorrow and planning intelligently for them.

And then I proceeded:

How can you know where you're going if you don't know where you've been? That question is basic. Yet it grieves me to continually meet good, well intentioned resource professionals inadequately grounded in the history of their own fields: foresters who know little of Gifford Pinchot, landscape architects and park people barely acquainted with Frederick Law Olmsted, wildlifers ignorant of C. Hart Merriam and Ding Darling, and toxicologists who have never read *Silent Spring*.

Perhaps the inadequacy is no accident. America, after all, is ever the land of grand illusions, where it's easier to avoid the past, or to look at it as a pretty picture book, or a gala musical like "Oklahoma," complete with song, dance and happy-ending romance. However, as Thomas Merton warned in *Conjectures of a Guilty Bystander*, a myth is apt to become a daydream and the daydream an evasion.

Myths rationalize bigotry, exploitation, homelessness, hunger, war, and the degradation of the environment. For four hundred years, the dominant European/American policy toward the indigenous peoples of this country has been one of continuous genocide. And the same for indigenous animals. Even now the grizzly bear is widely regarded as a "savage killer." Snakes are "slimy," although their skin is actually very dry; the coyote is "cowardly," the mountain lion "ravenous and craven." The South was long a mythic paradise all its own, in which benevolent, cultured planters loved and protected slaves, those innocent, joyful, songful "darkies." Merton wrote that the word "frontier" began as the symbol of adventure and clear-eyed innocence but acquired pathetic overtones in Kennedy's "new frontier," trying to keep the myth alive, rather than recognize that America had become prisoner of the curse.

It may be difficult to picture a culture, or a nation like ours, as "prisoner of the curse," and yet modern America is the victim of a syndrome that glorifies greed, that pervades and weakens government and all our institutions and professions. Little wonder that priorities are lopsided. The world spends $1.7 million a minute on military forces and equipment, $800 billion per year. The United States, in particular, has spent vast sums for "security," with illegal and immoral acts in other countries while, with a fraction of the amount, it could have given humanitarian aid and eliminated the threat of war.

Something is out of whack in a country that spends more than a billion dollars for a telescope while failing to care for its hungry; that cannot help its mentally ill; that crowds its prisons and condemns the imprisoned to defeat, dependence, and despair.

"A nation that continues year after year to spend more money on military defense than on programs of social uplift is approaching spiritual death," wrote Martin Luther King.

Society needs transformation – a viewpoint of human concern, distress and love. I feel we need a revolution of ideals, a revolution of ideas in all fields, a revolution of ethics to sweep America and the world. We must, for one thing, alter the lifestyle that makes us enemies of ourselves, a lifestyle that confuses a standard of living with the quality of life. That, however, may be the simplest part. Each of us who wants to make a difference must understand more about the history of ideas that dominate the philosophy and policy of society, that dictate our obsession with facts and figures, more about the analytical type of thinking of western science that provides power over nature while smothering us in ignorance about ourselves as part of it.

I wish I could cite education as the answer, but education as we know it is about careers, jobs, success in a materialistic world. It's about elitism, rather than about caring and sharing. It's about facts and figures, cognitive values, rather than about feeling derived from the heart and soul. It's about conformity, being safe in a structured society, rather than about questioning and restructuring society.

Education has become part of the problem instead of the solution. During the recent summer I read an Associated Press report on campus racism. It showed that many schools have established programs to deal with bigotry, but they are for the most part tokens without genuine commitment or understanding behind them. That isn't surprising. Consider that when the world was created it had a certain unity to it. The world was incomplete, to be sure, and changing, even as it is now, but the parts all fit, each part contributing to the advancement of the earth. But today the human components, presumably the most sophisticated of God's creatures, work against each other: rich against poor, men against women, straight versus gay, old versus young, black against white, Gentile against Jew, Moslem against Hindu, physically and mentally able against the disabled, the educated versus the uneducated.

It shouldn't be that way, considering that we are all sisters and brothers, born of the same Mother Earth, derived from the same living substance manifest in creation of the earth. But education too often is not a unifying influence. It tends to divide individuals and to repress respect for individuality. The straight A student is the paragon. Straight A means the student is honored and regarded by parents, while the student who brings home less – because, perhaps, he or she perceives magic in butterflies or beetles – becomes a family problem. The level of talent is externally defined, even though life itself is the essence of talent.

The thought of reversing course may seem unrealistic and intimidating, but as Willis Harmon wrote in *Global Mind Change*, "No economic, political or military power can compare with the power of a change of mind. By deliberately changing their internal image of reality, people are changing the world. First we must be willing to get rid of the poisonous beliefs that have led to the state of affairs as they exist at present."

In this same vein, but more pertinent to the individual, I will cite an interview with Brian Willson, which appeared in the illuminating pacifist publication, *Fellowship*. You may remember Brian Willson as the nonviolent protester who in September 1987 sat on the tracks to block a train carrying weapons to Central America and lost both legs. In the interview, titled "The Road to Transformation," Brian explains that his disenchantment began as a lieutenant in Vietnam. Later he went to Nicaragua and began networking with people to explore ways of expressing individual conscience. By working to extricate himself from what he considers a complicity of madness, Brian underwent a healing process and intense personal transformation. He concluded:

> Nonviolence is not so much a tactic as a way of experiencing the world within yourself, of understanding the sacred connection with all of life. It's an understanding of how everything is interconnected and how everything is in a state of interrelationship. We are going against our own nature when we start disrespecting all the other parts of life: people, plants, animals, water, sunlight, clouds. I think nonviolence is an attitude and way of life with a spiritual ecological dimension that is aware of how everything is interconnected and responds honestly to that.

Yes, *Spiritus et Materia Unum*: the antithesis between the material world and the spirit simply does not exist, since the material world is only the content of the spirit. To recognize this idea is the most important discovery of a lifetime, enriching and empowering the individual to do what he or she believes to be right, regardless of consequences. I love the words of John Trudell, the Indian leader, at the 1980 Black Hills Survival Gathering:

> We must go beyond the arrogance of human rights. We must understand natural rights, because all the natural world has a right to exist. The energy and the power of the elements – that is, the sun and the wind and the rain – is the only real power. There is no such thing as military power; there is only military terrorism. There is no such thing as economic power; there is only economic exploitation. That is all it is. We are an extension of the Earth, we are not separate from it. The Earth is spirit and we are an extension of that spirit. We are spirit. We are power.

John's words are rich and challenging, calling those who hope to heal the earth to join with those who hope to heal the souls of humankind to bring something new to a society in distress. They underscore lessons of history, including current history, still to be learned. For example, despite brief periods of concern or support for the native peoples, there has never been a mass movement of non-Indians demanding that our government honor its treaties and grant them basic rights of autonomy and self-determination. The tribal council system was imposed by the United States government in 1930 to replace the traditional leadership that would not sign away their lands to oil and mineral companies.

Likewise, the Alaska Native Settlement Claims Act of 1971 was designed not to benefit natives but to open the North Slope for oil development. Now, under the guise of settling a fabricated Hopi-Navajo land dispute, our government and both tribal councils have been trying to force traditional people from their land to clear the way for coal strip mines and other mineral exploitation. At the heart of the Indians' struggles for their land and their way of life is the understanding that this must be a spiritual struggle.

I urge interpreters to embrace the spiritual struggle and to face the issues of the troubled world. Though nuclear weapons will never force nations to join in recognizing the limits of a fragile earth, environmental interpreters can lead in pledging allegiance to a green and peaceful planet. I realize that this isn't easy, but the individual with conscience and courage will find the way.

For example, my friend Gilbert Stucker made his first visit to Dinosaur National Monument, along the Colorado-Utah border, in 1953 completely on his own, not primarily as a professional paleontologist but as a citizen preservationist deeply concerned with proposals to construct two dams across the rivers within the national monument. Like many others, he feared that allowing such a project in Dinosaur would place the entire national park system in jeopardy. Gil encouraged the Park Service to develop the dinosaur quarry as a positive project, displaying and interpreting dinosaur remains while at the same time interesting the public in the surrounding canyons and the threats to them. Presently, as the project got underway, he was offered, and accepted, a temporary appointment as ranger-naturalist. Visitors would ask questions, giving him the chance to lecture to large and small groups.

"I realized full well that when I discussed the proposed dams, I was exceeding my authority," Gil recalled later, "I was supposed to explain the quarry to the visiting public, not ask people to write their congressmen. At one point the park superintendent called me into his office and said, 'I just had a telegram from the Secretary of the Interior directing that no Park Service employee is to discuss the threat of dams in Dinosaur National Monument. I know you've been talking against the dams. If you continue, I will have to separate you or discharge you. I have no choice.'

"But I knew that I must talk against the dams and somehow rode it through until the question was settled and Dinosaur was saved."

Another example: One morning at Gatlinburg, Tennessee, in 1966 the Tennessee Commissioner of Conservation testified in support of the dreadful transmountain road across the Great Smoky Mountains as conceived and proposed by the director of the National Park Service. That very afternoon a young state park interpretive naturalist, Mack Prichard, testified as a private individual against the road. Some years later I asked Mack if he considered his independent action fitting and proper. He responded: "No, I don't think it was fitting. It was pretty risky, in fact. I felt if it cost me my job it was worth it – being honest about the fact I thought it was a lousy idea. You do what you have to do sometimes. I thought it was a sorry idea to build another road. The park would be better off without the road it's got. Then you'd have twice as much wilderness."

You do what you have to do sometimes, because your career is a mission, not a job, and there's something bigger in life than a paycheck. In 1987, when I spoke at the University of Wisconsin-Green Bay, a graduate student told me of applying for a position as a summer naturalist at a camp for children operated by the Wisconsin Department of Natural Resources. On the application form he pondered one particular question, "Would you approve the use of pesticides?" He wondered whether to play it safe or to answer with his true feeling. He chose to respond that he would not approve the use of pesticides, a response that stirred hostility in his interview for the job. "You mean," he was asked, "you would not use a pesticide even if the children were threatened with poison ivy?" "No," my friend replied. "I would much rather explain poison ivy to the children." He didn't get the job, though he would have made an excellent naturalist, the kind that is most needed. But I'm sure he's doing something else rewarding and fulfilling.

My friend Alfred Runte, the historian, while working as an interpreter in Yosemite National Park during the summer of 1980, talked to visitors about national park ethics and ideology. He would begin by asking his audience to recognize that national parks are in jeopardy, then adding:

"What would you be willing to do to see that national parks remain part of the fabric of American society for generations to come? Would you give up some power so that geothermal development would not destroy Old Faithful? Would you use less lighting at home so that strip mines and coal-fired power plants would not be needed in the Southwest?"

For his troubles Runte was directed to a week of "rehabilitation training," if you can imagine that for a scholar and university professor. He took it all in and subsequently delivered his message as he chose. Runte's travail, however, was not over. Brilliant historian and masterful teacher though he may be, he was denied tenure at the University of Washington. But when one door closes another will open, as evidenced by Alfred Runte's successful new book, *Yosemite, The Embattled Wilderness.* He learned that a program, any program, whether in a university or a public setting, without a theme, a message, is pointless. Dispensing information for information's sake is not what the National Park Service, or any interpreter in it, ought to be doing.

This leads me to mention a recent letter from a Western Washington University alumnus about his resignation from the National Park Service. "I used to love this job," wrote Chuck. "I can't begin to tell you what a difficult decision it was," but the politics imposed upon professionals working in the national parks got to be too much for him.

I felt disturbed and wrote the regional director. I wrote that I was not really surprised at the departure of a caring and competent person. I told the regional director that I had lately been to Mount Rainier, where the Paradise visitor complex was like a tourist ghetto. One evening I attended an interpretive program. The subject was listed as "Wilderness," but the interpreter knew little if anything about the Wilderness Act of 1964, one of the great landmark laws in the history of conservation, or about the National Wilderness Preservation System; the program on "Wilderness" was disappointing and dismal. The next day I heard one seasonal interpreter endeavor to discuss the status of the spotted owl, the symbol of our vestigial Northwest forests. But another seasonal called him aside with a reprimand, "You know very well that our superiors have instructed us to avoid controversy."

I did, in fact, receive, a courteous and considerate response to my letter from the regional director:

"Many of us agree with you that Chuck is a dedicated and competent employee. He has been recognized by the National Park Service through special awards and as the nominee of the Region for the Freeman Tilden Award, the highest honor in NPS interpretation." Then he went on, "Poorly trained seasonals certainly exist in the NPS, but from my own observations there are many permanents and seasonals alike who are passionately dedicated to wilderness and preservation values."

That's the tragedy of it: that caring people feel stressed and repressed by job restraints that keep them from speaking from the heart. Some have lost their chance for advancement, or rehire, or getting hired, by sticking to principle when expediency dictated otherwise. This must not be.

In 1968 I read an exciting article entitled "Concerning Dangers in National Parks," by an interpretive naturalist in the Everglades named Gale Zimmer. She was moved to express her viewpoint by the tragic death of two campers, who had been killed by grizzly bears in Glacier National Park. I have never met Gale, but read her article in a Park Service house organ. I would never find anything like it today, considering the Park Service publications stick close to the party line, thus are bland, sterile and sanitized.

Gale wrote:

> Maybe danger belongs in a national park. I think it's being there is what we mean by a "wilderness experience," a "national park experience." National parks are not cozy roadside tourist attractions, designed to satisfy the curiosity of mankind in padded comfort. They are slices of the natural world as they should be. And in the natural world there is "danger."
>
> People should know what a national park is – and isn't – before they commit themselves to spend their vacation or a weekend there. They should know if it's going to be rough and primitive and if they want the rough and primitive, fine. I think we have an obligation to inform people – honestly. But I think we betray the ideal behind the whole National Park System if we try to plane down all the rough spots, shoot all the touchy animals, fence off all the cliffs and offer visitors "a national park scene in the comfort of your own living room." With Thoreau I'd like to know an entire heaven and an entire earth, and I think basically our natural national parks should offer an entire heaven and an entire earth.

That's beautiful to me. I thank Gale for it, wherever she may be, and hope she may know her expression is not forgotten. The time is at hand, now more than ever, to speak openly, as she did. Those who give the most often don't get the recognition – that is true – but there is no limit to what you can accomplish as long as you don't care who gets the credit. Let us remember the words of Mark Twain: "To do good works is noble. To teach others to do good works is nobler, and no trouble."

Keynote address, National Association for Interpretation
Charleston, South Carolina, 1990

7. *Portrait of a conserver:*
Horace M. Albright

At the age of twenty-seven, Horace Marden Albright found himself appointed Acting Director of the National Park Service. His chief, Stephen T. Mather, was stricken with illness that would last a year. Young though he was in 1917, the Park Service itself was newly created and not one person, in Washington or anywhere in America, knew any more about running it than he.

The steps he took then and thereafter were giant in their dimensions, based on what he terms in retrospect "improvising and stubborn persistence." Within three years, Mount McKinley, Grand Canyon and Zion national parks were established, and so was the first one in the East, Lafayette in Maine, later renamed Acadia. The entire staff of the bureau originally consisted of Messrs. Mather, Albright and one stenographer. Now he faced the responsibility of finding office quarters, hiring personnel, handling the budget and complex legislation before Congress, and selling the principle of park protection to the public.

How he could have done all these things and design the foundation for a park system that is the envy of the world he seems to have explained himself in referring to the works of another American. "I do not believe they could have been done at all," wrote Mr. Albright of someone else's accomplishments, "without basic human compulsion to save what we prize for our fellows and for our children. He brings to the problems of conservation a natural love of the beauties of nature, an alert, inquiring mind, a realistic sense of pace and appropriateness."

Mr. Albright was describing with these words John D. Rockefeller, Jr., who for thirty-five years relied on his advice and judgment in spending countless millions to safeguard precious lands for public use. Without this relationship, it is highly unlikely that certain national parks would exist at all today, not the Great Smoky Mountains of the Southern Appalachians nor the Grand Tetons of the Wyoming Rockies nor the Virgin Islands in the Caribbean, nor portions of other parks. The beautiful gorge of Linville Falls in North Carolina, Mr. Rockefeller bought for $100,000 to be included in the Blue Ridge Parkway, virtually on Mr. Albright's say-so.

The protection of scenic beauty in national parks, however, represents only one phase of his career. The Albright touch is felt in regional and city planning through the pioneering work of the American Planning and Civic Association, of which he was president for a score of years. And so too in the movement to restore historic places, through his active concern long ago over George Washington's birthplace, Colonial Williamsburg, Jamestown Island, scenes where the story of a nation began. Few living men, if indeed any, have exercised a longer, or more profound, influence over the destiny of treasured American lands and landscape than Horace Albright. Though nearing the seventy-fifth anniversary of his birth in what might be called retirement in Los Angeles, he continues to be energized with ideas, activities and with helping others to extend the long trail he blazed. As one recipient of his generous assistance in time and inspiration, I know whereof I speak.

It is doubtless symbolic that he was born in 1890, the year the federal forest reserves were created, marking designation of portions of the public domain for protection in the public interest. His parents and grandparents were Nevada and California pioneers; as a boy in Inyo County he rode the High Sierra trails with forest rangers, learning about camping and packing in the wild country. In due course he went north to study economics and mining law at the University of California as a member of the class of 1912, in stimulating company, including [Earl Warren] the present chief justice of the United States; Newton B. Drury, later a director of the National Park Service, as well as of Save-the-Redwoods League; and Miss Grace Noble, who in 1965 will celebrate her fiftieth anniversary as Mrs. Horace Albright.

One year after graduation the young attorney went east to Washington in order to study mining and land laws on the scene where they are written. He joined the Department of Interior at a time when the few national parks already established were administered loosely by the old General Land Office, with protection provided on the ground not by rangers but by the Army. He was assigned to deal with legal matters concerning the parks; his duties shortly dovetailed with the movement led by the American Civic Association to provide these areas with a central administration. In 1915 when Mr. Mather became assistant to the secretary in charge of national parks, the two became intimate friends.

In those early years Assistant Director Albright was here, there, everywhere. In 1919 he became the first civilian Superintendent of Yellowstone, where the Army Corps of Engineers and cavalry units had been in charge since that Park was created in 1872. He spent summers in the field (he was credited with learning more about the Yellowstone wildlife and back country than any other person); then he returned to Washington in the winter to pick up legal and administrative problems of the whole park system.

In 1924, he and John D. Rockefeller, Jr., discovered each other, beginning their long period of association based on mutual respect and trust. The shy, wealthy gentleman of eastern parts arrived on tour of Yellowstone with his three oldest sons, John, Nelson and Laurance, to be greeted at the railroad depot by the park superintendent. At the moment of meeting, John III, eighteen, was recording in a notebook the amounts paid in tips to Pullman porters, while [Nelson Rockefeller] the present governor of New York, then sixteen, was engaged in helping the porters transfer baggage from the train to Yellowstone Park buses. Mr. Rockefeller was not unfamiliar with national parks, having earlier helped to acquire land at Acadia, in Maine, but this trip marked his full entry into philanthropy for conservation. Two years later, for example, he was back again and traveled with Mr. Albright from Yellowstone down to Jackson Hole, riding over an old wagon trail along the bluff overlooking the Snake River. It was an experience that resulted in his buying and donating land for the Grand Teton National Park. On the same trip he became interested in the redwoods of northern California, providing $2,000,000 to the Save-the-Redwoods League to purchase the famous Bull Creek Grove, later renamed by the California Park Commission as the Rockefeller Redwood Forest.

I had always thought that Mr. Albright's role at Colonial Williamsburg, the Rockefeller restoration project that began in this same period, was more academic than active. He served on the board of directors for twenty-four years almost from the very start. During a recent visit to Williamsburg I learned from Edwin Kendrew, the senior vice president, whose career spans its entire history, of the part played by Mr. Albright.

"Getting Williamsburg going was daring in its way, like plowing new ground. There was nothing like it in America, nor dreamed of," recalled Mr. Kendrew, who joined the project as chief draftsman. "But Mr. Rockefeller was not interested in restoring a single building in inappropriate surroundings – his objective was to revive an entire segment of the past or none at all. He was reticent, cautious, and kept largely to himself.

But Horace Albright was able to penetrate with sound advice in particularly trying areas – of principle, policy and ideals, and of spending money in the right places.

"Looking back, it is difficult to define Horace Albright's precise role at Williamsburg. He was helpful in zoning and city planning in our painstaking, slow endeavor – the battle to turn back the pages of history with authenticity. He supported the architects and other professionals in matters which some considered visionary, if not unnecessary, in the Twentieth Century context. One was the instance of setting the new hotel well back from the street. Or, he would tell Mr. Rockefeller that detailed research into the shape and substance of original buildings might be costly, but was essential. He championed purchase of land not only for restoration but for protection of the area from encroachment. 'It will never be any cheaper, you know,' he would suggest to Mr. Rockefeller. When it was proposed to intrude on history with modern street lights, he insisted that one concession would only lead to another. 'Instead of giving the visitor convenience,' he said on one occasion, 'we should give him a street map.'

"He could make his points stick, at Williamsburg and elsewhere, because he had a love for people at all stations, for a carpenter or gardener no less than for Laurance Rockefeller, whom he influenced deeply to take up his father's work in conservation. In time, when Congress passed the Historic Sites Act and the Park Service undertook its own restoration work, Washington people would say, 'Let's go down and see how the experts do it at Williamsburg.' That fine rapport was his work."

In 1928, when Stephen Mather was taken critically ill and resigned, Mr. Albright was named director of the Park Service. A curious thing was that he didn't seek the job, despite what is often said to be the bent of all who start climbing the bureaucratic ladders. But he once told me how Arno B. Cammerer, the associate director of the Service, demanded that he consider accepting the top position. "I did not want to be director, I wanted to stay at Yellowstone," Mr. Albright recalled. "Mr. Cammerer felt that he did not have the health to undertake leadership of the Service and, always loyal to his friends, myself included, he disclaimed any desire to be director; in fact, said he would refuse the appointment. Therefore, it seemed to me that sooner or later I would have to accept it, although I resisted the opportunity as long as I could."

His four years as director were a golden age. The Park Service turned its attention to preservation of historic sites, beginning with reconstruction of George Washington's birthplace at Wakefield, Virginia, then with the transfer of administration of military and battlefield parks from the War Department. Though he knew how to get things done in the halls of Congress and in the executive branch, from the White House on down, he established a level of respect for his bureau based on pride and non-partisan integrity. Politicians and promoters have always tried to obtain national park administration for their pet projects, regardless of their qualifications – it was far more difficult for them then than now.

A principal project of the early 1930's became the establishment of Great Smoky Mountains National Park, a marvelous half-million-acre Appalachian forest, much of it virgin wilderness, acquired for $10,000,000, one-half paid by the adjoining states of North Carolina and Tennessee, the other half by John D. Rockefeller, Jr.

In 1933, after twenty years in government service, Horace Albright resigned as director of the National Park Service to become general manager, and later president, of the U. S. Potash Company. His family were miners before him, he had studied mining law at Berkeley under one of the great experts, William E. Colby, and directing a large scale mining operation represented a new challenge, like starting afresh with a new bureau. Nevertheless, through the years of business, his influence in matters of conservation and parks did not wane. His headquarters in New York were only one building removed from those of John D. Rockefeller, Jr., in Rockefeller Center. He served the government on committees, commissions and boards. Members of Congress counted – and still count – on his wisdom and judgment. I attended a testimonial dinner in Washington last year for Senator Clinton Anderson, of New Mexico. That foremost conservationist and champion of wilderness legislation named Horace Albright among a half-dozen or so who had been most helpful to him over the decades in Washington.

Mr. and Mrs. Albright live today within a long stride of the UCLA campus, partially because one of his current activities is membership on the Council of the Friends of the UCLA Library. And not by accident; books are a passion, filling shelves from floor to ceiling in almost every room of his house, including the basement, an amazing collection, carefully arranged to reflect the study of his special interests – the life and times of Theodore Roosevelt, mining, forestry, wildlife, the national parks, the California story. A prize package if ever there was one, which, together with his correspondence and scrapbooks, must surely compare in value with the

Gifford Pinchot collection presently available to scholars at the Library of Congress in Washington and must deserve some similar future, perhaps at headquarters of the National Park Service.

"I have been submerged in correspondence," he wrote me last year, in scorn of the temptations of age to live at ease. "I do not expect to be in the East anytime soon. Normally, I would be there in October for the meeting of directors of Resources for the Future, but Mrs. Albright and I are planning a trip to Nairobi, Kenya, for the International Union for the Conservation of Nature." And another time, "We have lately been to Owens Valley, where I was born and reared. As a trustee of the National Trust for Historic Preservation, I was asked to make the address at the annual dinner of the Eastern California Museum Association. So we went up there and stayed a few days to enjoy the beauty of the mountains covered with a mantle of snow."

In his lifetime, he has been associated with scores of good causes, in the East, the Hudson River Conservation Society, Palisades Interstate Park Commission, the Theodore Roosevelt Association and American Scenic and Historic Preservation Society; elsewhere with the American Pioneer Trails Association, National Conference on State Parks, Jackson Hole Preserve, the Museum of Navajo Ceremonial Art in New Mexico; in his own state, with efforts to establish Kings Canyon National Park, to save Hetch Hetchy Valley in Yosemite, the South Calaveras Grove of Big Trees and with the Save-the-Redwoods League. Honors have come to him from the government of Sweden, Garden Club of America, the Sierra Club and his alma mater, which named him Alumnus of the Year in 1952, plus many others.

Yet, in this summary of a great man's career, it should be noted that he has not always been above criticism. In the early years of the National Parks he supported public feeding of grizzly bears at Yellowstone and the "Rock of Ages singing" at Carlsbad Caverns, which verge more on entertainment than park conservation and are no longer practiced – though perhaps they were right in the context of their time. So too with the peculiar placement and design of Jackson Lake Lodge in Grand Teton National Park, a disconsonant obstacle in the path of one of America's noblest views; but this, I venture, was Mr. Rockefeller's choice, based on his own ideas and the prerogative of his millions of dollars invested in protecting Jackson Hole.

I think of Mr. Albright's own words that the mission of conserving the best of America takes many forms of expression in different individuals, and that the real requirement is "wider support from more citizens who will take the trouble to inform themselves of new needs and weak spots in our conservation program." No man has done better to show the way to his own generation, or done more to inspire a succeeding generation. In his fearless, fighting days in Washington, a crusty old Senator [Kenneth McKellar, of Tennessee] once hailed him to Capitol Hill to demand construction of a road where wilderness belonged. When Parks Director Albright refused to acquiesce, the Senator exploded, vilified his parentage and had to be restrained physically. That road, however, was not built. The qualities of courage and conviction, derived from his love of the land, have characterized the life of Horace Albright. The nation will everlastingly be richer for his coming our way.

From *Westways*, 1964

8. A man of the parks:
Newton B. Drury

The first time I met Newton B. Drury he impressed me as a man of poise and class and that was definitely not on one of his better days. It was in the spring of 1951, at a luncheon in Washington only hours after the newspapers had reported his forced resignation as director of the National Park Service. He looked a little pained as though smiling through the tears, but only a little. The larger expression was of pride in a tough battle lost and of determination that the war over the principle at stake must be won.

The principle he defended was sustained. Director Drury had resisted plans to construct dams in national parks and had been forced out, but the dams were not built, and he successfully demonstrated that America's natural sanctuaries could be held inviolate, come what may.

Newton Drury during his long life (which ended at the age of 89 in December, 1978) was many things, but a preservationist above all. With the passing of time I feel sure that his stature will grow, with recognition extending far beyond those who already know of him and his work. The cathedral groves of redwood trees in the moisture-rich coastal fog belt along the Pacific Coast are part of his legacy, reflecting his years at the helm of the Save-the-Redwoods League. And so, too, the network of national parks, often cited as a model of preservation to the rest of the world.

But maybe it's the concepts he embodied that count most: the ideas that people can actually save big things seemingly beyond reach, then protect them without compromise or sacrifice. As he himself said, with typical clarity while fending off one threat to the national parks after another, "Civilization is encroaching on the wilderness all over the land. What remains of it becomes increasingly precious."

Drury came by his concerns and career logically and naturally. He was born in San Francisco of pioneer California parents. His father, Wells Drury, was a prominent Western journalist. While attending Berkeley High School, Newton was a dance band cornetist, but once he entered college

– the University of California, naturally – he switched to journalism, debating, and campus politics. In his senior year Drury was elected president of the student body, no small feat in the celebrated Class of 1912, which included Horace M. Albright, Newton's intimate friend then and thereafter, and another friend, Earl (Pinky) Warren.

Following graduation Drury remained for a time at the university as administrative assistant to the president and lecturer in English literature. However, he had a rendezvous to keep with his younger brother, Aubrey, a talented journalist and travel writer. Together they opened a San Francisco public relations firm, the Drury Company, and proceeded to assemble prestigious clients, like the Mark Hopkins Hotel, and likely could have spent their lives as successful and profitable image builders.

The redwoods interposed to change things. Taller than the first "skyscrapers" rising over the landscape of New York, the coastal redwoods, *Sequoia sempervirens*, in the early years of the century still reached in glorious groves from the Oregon border to Big Sur. But they were in private hands and endangered as timber too valuable for their own good. Hoping to reverse the prevalent logging trend, prominent Californians and national figures of note discussed organizing a public organization to be called Save-the-Redwoods League. Among those sparking the movement were Stephen T. Mather, who in 1916 had become first director of the National Park Service, and his young assistant, Albright, along with Henry Fairfield Osborn, John C. Merriam, and Madison Grant. When it came to getting things rolling these luminaries turned to Newton Drury.

He was the man for the job; or perhaps I should say he and his brother were the men for the job. From the time the League was founded in 1919 until 1978 the history of the League and careers of Newton and Aubrey were virtually synonymous. As a matter of record, they would in time put together thirty magnificent redwood state parks comprising 135,000 acres.

Newton became the first executive secretary. He prepared the League's articles of incorporation and launched a PR and fund-raising campaign in behalf of his clients, the trees. Over the years he conducted an eminently successful effort to enroll members and assemble donations for acquisition of virgin redwood forests. He became known for his guided tours of the Redwood Empire, on which he would induce citizens of means to purchase specific groves as living memorials. His guests would include, in 1926, Mr. and Mrs. John D. Rockefeller, Jr., and three of their sons, leading to the gift of two million dollars to buy the magnificent Bull Creek Grove in Humboldt Redwoods State Park.

Plainly here was a case of effective citizen action through an independent private organization. But it pointed up the need of a government role as well, if indeed the redwoods were to be saved and maintained for public good. Thus in 1928 Californians voted to support a state bond issue providing for matching funds derived from public contributions. This unique arrangement of public-private partnership marked the making of California's state park system. From the inception Drury served as acquisition officer, putting the new parks together, through the terms of four different governors.

He continued to fill his singular role in California until 1940, when he was induced to come to Washington as the fourth director of the National Park Service, following Mather, Albright, and Arno B. Cammerer. Aubrey, meanwhile, took over as secretary of the Save-the-Redwoods League so the Drury connection there remained unbroken.

Secretary of the Interior Harold L. Ickes, the cantankerous self-styled curmudgeon, appointed Drury as director (he had wanted him even earlier) and stood behind him when need be, much to Ickes' credit, considering that Drury was a Republican serving in a Democratic administration. In 1940, however, war was coming on. To make room for defense agencies, the Park Service and other bureaus were shipped to Chicago, rather like being placed in cold storage, leaving only a skeleton liaison staff in Washington. Though for five years his headquarters was out of the main arena, the director faced a barrage of demands and challenges. Throughout the war the parks were under pressure; repeated proposals called for sacrificing one or another to the war effort, for the installation of equipment on mountaintops, or for military maneuvers, or for logging and mining.

Conrad L. Wirth, who later succeeded Drury as director, recalls how things went: "We could not have had a better man at the head of our bureau during those trying times. I saw him in conferences when he would answer these proposals by saying, 'If you can bring a statement from the secretary of your department saying the war absolutely depends on exploiting a national park, we might give in.'" As a consequence, little damage was done to the parks, and none of it needlessly.

Following the war, new threats arose. Commercial interests brought political pressure to open Olympic National Park to mining and logging.

They demanded access to national monuments, including Saguaro, Organ Pipe Cactus, Death Valley, Joshua Tree, and Glacier Bay. The Bureau of Reclamation and Army Corps of Engineers discovered potential in parks for water power, flood control, and irrigation and proposed projects in Big Bend, Glacier, Grand Canyon, Kings Canyon, and Mammoth Cave.

"If we are going to succeed in preserving the greatness of the national parks, they must be held inviolate," Drury insisted in resisting the rationale that scenic and recreational resources could be used for other purposes without sacrificing their implicit values. He believed the most rewarding and inspiring experiences derive from primeval nature as safeguarded in national parks. "They represent the last stands of primitive America. If we are going to whittle away at them we should recognize, at the very beginning, that all such whittlings are cumulative and that the end result will be mediocrity."

It was a golden era for the National Park Service. The agency under Drury was guided by principle and idealism rather than by politics or expediency. I recall how, even years later, parks people of that day were proud to identify themselves as "Drury men."

Drury stuck to his guns in opposing two dams which the Bureau of Reclamation, a sister agency at Interior, wanted to build in Dinosaur National Monument. In June 1950, Secretary Oscar Chapman (who succeeded Ickes) announced his support for the dams. The following spring he removed Drury. Actually, Newton was given a choice of becoming governor of distant Samoa or a special assistant to the Secretary without anything special to do. His only real option was to resign, which he did with dignity and class.

Washington's loss was California's gain. Governor Earl Warren, his old classmate, forthwith appointed him director of California's Division of Beaches and Parks, which he had been instrumental in establishing years before. What a network these parks now constitute! The system embraces natural areas from the Anza-Borrego desert to redwood rain forests, beach parks along the Southern California coast where so sorely needed, and historic parks recounting virtually every phase in human history, including homes of figures like Jack London and Will Rogers, and the San Simeon castle of William Randolph Hearst.

In 1959, Newton reached the state's mandatory retirement age of 70. His brother died the same year, so he picked up where Aubrey left off, serving again as executive secretary of the League, then later as president and chairman. In June 1979, six months following Newton's passing, a substantial grove at Prairie Creek Redwoods State Park was dedicated to the memory of both brothers.

Assuredly the very existence of the Drury Grove will spread hope and inspiration the world over. That is one way to look at it, but there is still another. The aspiration of every writer is to evoke something of merit in his own lifetime that may outlast it. Newton Drury was literate, as well as refined and essentially modest. His old friend, Horace Albright, should have the last word on what Drury did and stood for. Those two differed at times on the approach, but never on their common goal in conservation.

"He could have written extensively," Horace said some years ago, "but he dedicated his life to saving and protecting primitive, unspoiled features of America's heritage – not by words alone, but by deeds."

Cosmos Club Bulletin, 1980; *Living Wilderness,* 1980.

9. A kind of special breed:
Conrad L. Wirth

Directors of the National Park Service are a kind of special breed. They have been few in number, though it now requires the fingers of more than one hand to count all who have guided the destiny of their service since its birth in 1916. If I were to choose one director to symbolize the spirit of the entire group from Stephen T. Mather, the founding father, down through Conrad L. Wirth, it might very well be Arno B. Cammerer, who served from 1933 to 1940, when he suffered a heart attack under the pressures of his position, then voluntarily stepped down to become a regional director until his death two years later. "His love of the work was too great," declared Congressman Edward T. Taylor soon after in a memorial address on the floor of the House of Representatives.

"His love of the work was too great." This sentence binds together the breed of park service directors, applying to one as it does to all – certainly no less to Conrad Louis Wirth, who is retiring in January, 1964, after twelve years as director, and a full thirty-five years of government employment, than to his predecessors whose names already have been inscribed in the record books of parks and the conservation movement.

I first met Connie Wirth in 1951, on the North Carolina section of the Blue Ridge Parkway, shortly before his appointment. Down through the years I saw him many times, out in the parks and in Washington, and learned to know him well. Looking through the files, I find the record of his first discussion of Mission 66 – even before the historic program of his term was given a name – at a dinner meeting I attended in December, 1954. It seemed fitting, therefore, soon after his retirement was announced, to call on Mr. Wirth, in order to review his years in office, the high spots and low spots, to learn why he chose this particular time to step down and his plans for the future.

Essentially, he seemed much like the same younger man I had encountered in North Carolina thirteen years earlier, buoyant, outgoing, imbued with the soundness of his cause – the classic career spirit of the National

Park Service that has made this agency a great force in American life. The only surface difference appeared to be in the thinned out hair of his head and the abundance of awards, decorations, diplomas and mementoes adorning the walls and tables of his office. As we talked, however, it developed that he had not only mellowed with the years, and grown more reflective, but voluntarily conceded instances when he had been wrong.

But in his thirty-five years there are far more rights than wrongs to weigh in the balance, lasting contributions in recreation and resource protection. He chose to mention three of these of which he is particularly proud and, curiously, two of them deal with broader fields than national parks alone.

The first dates to the early 1930s, soon after he joined the National Park Service, when he was asked by Horace M. Albright, who was then director, to supervise activities of the Civilian Conservation Corps in state parks. Three years later, his responsibility was broadened. Arno Cammerer, who succeeded Mr. Albright, assigned him to take charge of CCC work in the national parks as well, and Secretary Harold L. Ickes appointed him to represent the Interior Department on the overall CCC advisory council. Interior had 500 camps out of a total of 1500.

"It was a period of great increase in funds and development, which really had its start with President Hoover's authorization to build roads in Shenandoah National Park," Mr. Wirth said. "We went great guns in the thirties. In fact, many facilities constructed by the CCC are still in use.

"The Park Service even earlier had been closely associated with state park development. As early as 1921, Stephen Mather was instrumental in establishing the National Conference on State Parks. In the CCC period, many states organized park systems for the first time in order to qualify for federal funds. At their request, we wrote legislation for systems in nineteen states, which had no parks at all or only one or two. During the ten years of CCC, state parks accomplished what they normally would have done in fifty years."

This led to the second highlight of his career, initiating the Park, Parkway and Recreation Study Act of 1936, which provided for cooperative planning with the states.

"In a sense," Mr. Wirth said, "this act laid the groundwork for the present Bureau of Outdoor Recreation. We worked together with no less than forty-three of the forty-eight states. It sparked the state park planning program.

"There was another aspect of the program under which we acquired submarginal lands to develop for recreation purposes. Most were within fifty miles of big cities, like Prince William Park in Virginia and Catoctin in Maryland, part of which is now the President's retreat. It was built by the Park Service in 1941 with CCC and special funds for Franklin D. Roosevelt as his famous 'Shangri-la'; now, of course, it's known as Camp David. Forty-eight of these parcels were demonstration areas, purchased by the federal government and then given to the states.

"I remember how we were prohibited by law from paying over $10 an acre on the average. To balance out the high cost of land around the cities, we acquired a large tract cheaply on the Little Missouri River near Medora in the Badlands of North Dakota. Ultimately it turned out to be a fine acquisition in its own right, because of the unusual landscape, wildlife and association with Theodore Roosevelt. It is now the Theodore Roosevelt National Memorial Park [later to be reclassified as a national park]."

His third high point of pride, of course, is Mission 66. Though he prefers to share credit for the program with associates in the Park Service, all agree the concept was his alone.

How was Mission 66 born?

"When I became director in 1951," he said, "I marveled at how Newton B. Drury, my predecessor, had kept things going through trying times. During the years of World War II, the number of visitors had dropped to about five million from about twenty-one million in 1941, the last pre-war year. The regular appropriations were cut seventy-five percent while the special funds – such as CCC and WPA – were gone completely. In 1946, total travel to the parks was up again to twenty-one million and continued to rise rapidly from there on. But the government paid very little attention, being preoccupied with the Cold War and military police actions. In every respect, the parks were deteriorating; we faced a fantastic backlog of repairs. We were operating on a year-to-year basis, unable to catch up, let alone to project for future needs."

I recall a statement Mr. Wirth prepared in late 1954 on the many-sided problems of the parks. Nearly every campground, he reported then, was subject to excessive damage because of continuous overuse. Roads and trails were in ill repair. Overnight accommodations were insufficient in number and, in many cases, inadequate in quality. Private landholdings within parks obstructed maintenance and sound administration, and the parks faced the threat of real estate subdivisions inside their boundaries.

At least half the housing for park personnel was substandard, aged and obsolete. The statement declared:

> Growing crowds of visitors, numbering forty-six million in 1953, intensify the problem of protecting the parks. Many park features are irreplaceable and are subject to vandalism and theft. These must be continually protected if future generations are to enjoy them. Park museum collections are housed in structures that must be protected from fire. Fires may be caused by both lightning and careless acts of man, the risk from the latter increasing in proportion to the increase of visitors and lack of protection personnel. Management of the large wildlife population is an added risk.

It was time to do something, something dramatic, before the parks fell apart at the seams in disrepair and their unprotected features fell from the pedestal of magnificence into obscurity under the weight of visitor numbers. "Congress had the right to know how much it would cost to restore the National Park System to a standard the American people expected of it," he told me. "So we devised a broad program that outlined present conditions; estimated the cost to replace worn, outmoded facilities; provided for additional new ones to meet present and anticipated requirements, and prepared a fiscal timetable that would accomplish these objectives in the most economical way. It turned out to be a ten-year program. We then set our sights to complete it by 1966. It became a service-wide mission, Mission 66. When people asked, 'What do you mean?," it automatically gave us the opportunity to explain it to them."

But he stressed that Mission 66 has not been a program of construction alone. Inherent is protection, of the visitor, of natural features, wilderness and wildlife. During the first seven years of Mission 66, more money was made available for acquiring private inholdings than in the entire preceding history of the Park Service.

Interpretive developments, museum displays, roadside exhibits and guided trails came to the fore, affording an experience of quality to the vast number of park visitors. The "visitor center," a direct outgrowth of Mission 66, became a new term in the travel lexicon, a focal point where the visitor can obtain information on the specific area around him or any other part of the National Park System. It has since set a pattern adapted to other federal agencies and many states. In addition, new areas in the early days of Mission 66, including Minuteman National Historic Park,

Cape Cod, Padre Island and Point Reyes National Seashores, have been added to the National Park System.

There is no doubt that Mission 66 has been a landmark program in the management of natural resources, as well as one of the greatest personal achievements of any federal official in the history of conservation.

On the other hand, Connie Wirth has not always been a hero to all people. He has faced some tough issues – proposals to build dams in some parks and to open others to public hunting. He has been subject to criticism from all directions. From commercial tourist operators, ski promoters and road builders demanding greater development of facilities. From some conservation organizations, insisting on the sanctity of wilderness preservation, and objecting strenuously to construction of roads such as the one across Tioga Pass to Yosemite.

"That was a hard decision," he said. "The location and design had been studied and recommended over a long period of time by many experts, including Frederick Law Olmsted, the great landscape architect. I decided to accept that recommendation. When you drive over it, I think you will agree it's one of the truly fine roads of the National Park System. It does cut across a portion of glacial polish, to be sure, but I don't believe we opened or destroyed wilderness. To the contrary, we've given people a chance to look into wilderness.

"To one person, climbing the Teton peaks is an inspiring experience, while to another driving along the Snake River and looking up at the mountains holds the same appeal. My basic idea has been that parks are for people – for people to use and enjoy, but not with the right to abuse or destroy. The biggest problem has been, and will continue to be, convincing the public of the need for sound management, protection and preservation."

Mr. Wirth was not hesitant to note that he had made mistakes on occasion. "Of course, I have." he said. "Every director will make honest errors of judgment. But if it wasn't too late, I tried to correct mine as best I could."

We talked about mistakes. One was his early attitude toward the proposal to create a Bureau of Outdoor Recreation. He said that his position was misunderstood. "It is true that at first I felt the Park Service should handle recreation planning, as we have done since 1936," he told me. "I was wrong. On further study, I reached the conclusion that an operating bureau should not handle over-all planning. To have an agency of government designed specifically for planning purposes is eminently sound. It has the quality of objectivity that we might lack. Certainly we have no monopoly on recreation and nothing gives me greater pleasure than to see other federal agencies play their part in the picture."

He regretted also the seeming friction between the Park Service and Forest Service, which became particularly acute following the conference of park superintendents at Williamsburg four years ago, when he was quoted as "throwing down the gauntlet." I mentioned how such expressions complicated the lives of those who admire both services.

"That was unfortunate," he replied. "We had the wrong impression of the Forest Service program of multiple use, or multiple benefits. Our relations with the Forest Service today are fine and firm. I'm glad to see it moving ahead in the recreation field. No doubt we are going to have disagreements on specific questions, but these can be resolved on the basis of cooperation between sister agencies. We want to see more recreation development on public lands at all levels of government – national forests, state parks, and the state forests, which are virtually unexplored. The more they can do to provide people with the good outdoor life, the more the national parks can succeed in preserving their priceless, spectacular natural and historic features.

"Every agency feels the pressure of public use and demand. We get almost one hundred million visitors a year, the national forests even more, the state parks three hundred million. Though each fills a different purpose, we share common problems. This is particularly true of the Park Service and Forest Service, which, in the final analysis, stand or fall together. Park and forest rangers out on the ground every day in the year prove that cooperation between the agencies is practiced in more than words."

Now the question arose in our conversation as to why he chose this particular time to retire. The unfortunate fact is that a gloomy pall was cast over the announcement last October of his decision to step down. It appeared to many observers that he had been forced out by higher officials of the Department of the Interior. While Secretary Stewart Udall paid him tribute as "an outstanding public servant," Assistant Secretary John A. Carver, Jr. chose the occasion, at the superintendents conference in Yosemite, to excoriate the Park Service in no uncertain terms for a variety of "sins," including adherence to "a quasi-religious mystique."

There were other cloudy circumstances surrounding the event. Mr. Carver's speech, with its criticism of Mr. Wirth, found its way into several newspapers almost as it was being delivered. And when the official news release of his retirement was issued by the Interior Department, coupled to it was a report by the National Academy of Sciences calling for changes in administering Park Service research. This led the *Washington Post*, for one to advise its readers that "More criticism was heaped on the National Park Service as word of the retirement of its director, Conrad L. Wirth, became official." And the report of the National Academy of Sciences – though initiated over a year ago by the Park Service as one means of focusing attention on its need of research – became "the latest critical blast."

The truth is that all had not been harmony between the director of the National Park Service and higher echelons of the Department of the Interior. My understanding is that Secretary Udall and Mr. Wirth generally got along well, but that this condition did not carry over to relations with some of the Secretary's associates. Mr. Wirth declined forcefully to discuss with me issues of disagreement or to reply to Mr. Carver's criticisms, or to venture any criticism of his own on the indelicate circumstances of his retirement. I could not avoid the feeling, however, that here was a case where "His love of the work was too great".

His retirement was not forced, he insisted. It had been in his mind a long time in order to make way for younger men. His successor, George Hartzog, had been chosen one year ago. These, no doubt, are the facts of the case, though some questions remain to be answered. Secretary Udall, for example, has paid high tribute to Mr. Wirth and termed Mr. Carver's speech as "the sort of thing you do within the family as indicating you can do a better job in some fields." However, he has not yet explained the peculiar manner in which the speech, "within the family," became public – or whether he shares Mr. Carver's critical views of national park philosophy.

It is difficult to recognize that Conrad Wirth has reached the age of sixty-four. The words he used in his letter of retirement to characterize the National Park Service apply very much to him as an individual: "It is a vigorous, capable, aggressive and loyal organization, dedicated to serving the public in accordance with the objectives enacted into law by the Congress and the policies established by the administration and the Secretary of the Interior." As one who is vigorous, capable and aggressive, he could hardly be looking forward to easy years. He will be heard from; perhaps even by this time a new affiliation will have been announced.

"Call me a consultant," he suggested, "a man who has the latitude and freedom to undertake missions he considers important in fulfilling his own goals. I intend to plug for recognition of the professional in this field of conservation and recreation, for sound training of qualified people in protection of natural resources, for land acquisition at all levels of government. This country is just at the beginning of a great era in which parks will become far more priceless possessions than they have ever been, and when provisions for recreational opportunities, wherever possible, must become a requirement of all land agencies."

Certainly Director Wirth's contributions through the years have shaped both the role of the National Park Service and its public image. Before leaving, he allowed me to scan through a sheaf of hundreds of letters from well-wishers. These included scores from senators and congressmen. Through thirty years of appearances before committees on Capitol Hill, congressional relations became his long suit. He was most respected, I venture, because he played his hand for the national parks and public interest above board, free of political overtones or undertones. Of the letters I looked at, one expressed the feeling for Mr. Wirth shared by virtually all who have known him.

"It has been a pleasure to work with you," wrote Representative Wayne Aspinall, of Colorado, chairman of the House Interior Committee, "and to know that we had each other's confidence at all times, even though we had our differences, as well as our agreements, the latter being by far the most numerous and fruitful. You have rendered the nation and its people an outstanding service, a service which could only be the result of one whose whole being and energy are dedicated to the welfare of his fellow citizens. You are a great guy, a great public servant, and one who is loved by a legion of friends, among whom I am glad to be numbered."

American Forests, 1964

10. *Amazonia is worth more in its natural state*

On my first trip to South America I saw a land that was whole. That image is still vivid: of the unbroken forest, a "jungle," if you wish, endless and so thick my crewmates and I could barely see the streams flowing from the mountains and highlands to join other streams on their journey to the sea. In those days I was a young navigator in the Air Force (then the Army Air Corps), flying a transport mission across Venezuela, the Guianas, and the broad delta of the Amazon, eastward to the Brazilian bulge in the Atlantic, and from there to Africa.

That was almost fifty years ago, a brief flicker of time, but since then the world has turned upside down. All across the planet, seemingly impenetrable strongholds of nature have lost their defenses. In the four decades I have worked to recover those defenses by fighting for parks and reserves, I have learned that virtually anything set aside and saved reflects human restraint and deliberate design, the best side of modern civilization. For this reason I am pleased to contribute introductory words for William Leitch and his useful, pioneering *Guidebook to the National Parks of South America*, fittingly published by The Mountaineers as part of its mission "to explore, study, preserve and enjoy the natural beauty of the outdoors."

North Americans actually know little about the great continent to the south, as compared with the Caribbean, or Europe, or even Africa. Yet South America is a composite of wonderlands, extending 5,000 miles from the tropics almost to Antarctica. The Andean Cordillera, the longest continuous mountain range in the world, embraces forty-five peaks rising above 20,000 feet. Angel Falls, in the Guiana Highlands of Venezuela, is the highest waterfall in the world. Iguacu, the chain of falls along the border Argentina shares with Brazil and Paraguay, is higher than Victoria, twice as wide as Niagara, bordered by virgin forests bright with flowering plants, birds, and butterflies. At the southern tip of South America, the Strait of Magellan recalls the Inside Passage to Alaska and the Norwegian fjords, with snowy peaks and glaciers, rocky headlands, clouds and mists, and a life community where whales, porpoises and penguins outnumber people.

One part or another of South America provides home and habitat to marmoset and monkey, giant armadillo and anteater, the world's tiniest deer, maned wolf, mountain tapir, mountain lion, jaguar, ocelot, llama, and vicuna – plus bird life that includes the black-necked swan, cacique, condor, quetzal, flamingo, parrot and parakeet, toucan, trogan, and hundreds of species of dazzling and bizarre butterflies.

The survival of these species is no accident. Today these natural treasures of South America are located primarily within national parks, much like the treasures of the United States, and of countries all over the world, established through the initiative of individual citizens and the response of governments to their concern. The first national park in South America, as a case in point, was set aside in Argentina in 1903, from lands in Patagonia donated by Francisco "Perito" Moreno, who devoted his life to preserving Argentina's wild landscape. Where he began, others followed. In 1958, George Fulda, an executive of an Argentine travel agency, organized the Friends of the National Parks. In time he was joined by Dr. Maria Buchinger de Alitz, a professor of natural resource policy, who on a Guggenheim Fellowship had studied national parks in the United States. She then became a prime mover in organizing continent-wide seminars on natural areas and tourism.

South American parks are not as well developed as those in our country, and they are different, in general much more primitive, and for the most part poorly financed and understaffed. For these reasons, North Americans are well advised not to carry preconceived expectations with them to South America. Leitch carefully points out that visitors are often on their own, obliged to create their own park experiences. The serious park traveler will consider this an advantage rather than a liability, reading in advance and preparing carefully. *South America's National Parks* will prove invaluable with its details on climate and weather, visitor facilities, historical aspects, and glossaries of useful Spanish, Portuguese, and Dutch phrases.

The author and I believe that increased nature tourism will encourage countries to safeguard their treasures. Certainly Amazonia is worth more in its natural state to the eight countries sharing the river basin than if it was deforested and industrially developed. In 1978 I visited the Amazon mainstream at Manaus, 850 miles upriver from the Brazilian coast. I was astonished to find stretches of the river near the city lined with steel plants, power plants, microwave stations, logging mills, alcohol and petro-chemical complexes, and storage plants. In places it looked more like the Hudson River at Hoboken than a jungle river. On the other hand, I also saw pink fresh-water porpoises, birds and fish, and lovely *Victoria regia*, the meter-wide water lilies that symbolize the lush Amazon forest – a rain for-est with more types of plants, flowers, trees, birds, butterflies, reptiles, and mammals than any other forest on earth.

As scientists warn, stripping the Amazon forest cover can drastically alter the world's climate. Tourism can help to save it. Nevertheless, if tourism is an appropriate goal, it must be quality tourism worthy of the resource. That is what national parks are all about: protecting the setting and adjusting visitor use accordingly. Members of The Mountaineers and others who read this book will want it that way and can help make it so. This book will help readers to appreciate the sense of place, the purpose of place, the spirit of natural sanctuaries still largely undefiled. Once, at Rotorua, in New Zealand, an American woman told me how she had turned up the air conditioning and kept her windows closed all night to shut out the sound and smell of the geysers and other thermal features. She might as well have stayed home.

The way to see the national parks of South America – or national parks anywhere – is to travel simply, take nature as it comes, exult in it, and support the preservation of whatever can still be saved.

Foreword to *South America's National Parks*, by William C. Leitch, 1990.

11. The clock strikes twelve
for John Saylor

John P. Saylor is gone. He died last October 28 of heart failure, three months after celebrating his sixty-fifth birthday and after almost a quarter century in Congress. I cannot let him go without a farewell salute, for every reader of *Field & Stream*, indeed every American who enjoys and loves the outdoors, has lost a friend and champion.

His constituents in mountainous western Pennsylvania sent him to Washington for a total of twelve terms. Obviously he represented his district well in order to receive their continuing vote of confidence, especially as a Republican running in a predominantly Democratic area, but the truth is that he worked for a far broader constituency. He was a national congressman, a powerful, creative and effective force at the center of nearly every major conservation battle of the past twenty years.

Mr. Saylor's base of action was the House Committee on Interior Affairs, where, through the process of seniority, he became the ranking Republican member. I recall his commenting a number of years ago that, of about forty members on the committee, only six were from the East. There were absolutely no Easterners on the Senate Interior Committee. The Western power bloc in Congress, attuned to the voices of mining, oil, timber, grazing, water development and such special economic interests, had the Interior committees locked up in both houses.

"Western politics have long been imbued with the concept that natural resources are to be used profitably," Mr. Saylor noted. "One of the nice things about being an eastern member of the committee is that the Interior Department doesn't have anything in my district. The Forest Service doesn't have anything in my district either. I have no Indians in my district. I can look at propositions as they are presented and call them as I see them."

To call them as he saw them in behalf of the public interest was fundamental to him. Mr. Saylor had the courage to take strong, forthright and completely independent positions.

This was the genius of the man. Though a loyal Republican, he never hesitated to press his own views on a particular piece of legislation. His choice was always decided on the basis of principle, rather than partisanship, regardless of the consequences to himself.

I was privileged to enjoy a warm relationship with Mr. Saylor, or "Big John," as he was known among his colleagues in the House and his friends in Washington. He was a towering man, standing six-feet-four, robust and yet wiry, a vigorous, powerful presence in any group. He was blessed with sharp wit and sparkle, a willingness for combat. He may at times have appeared caustic, but I think this was a defensive cover that came from fighting so many battles against tough adversaries. After all, for years he was the counterbalancing influence in the House Interior Committee to Wayne Aspinall, the domineering Democratic chairman (who finally went down to defeat in the 1972 primary election).

As I knew Mr. Saylor, he was utterly fearless and tireless. He knew how to work within the system and believed in it. Hundreds of bills are introduced into each Congressional session, few are passed; but when you look at the landmark conservation legislation of the past two decades – including the Wilderness Act, Wild and Scenic Rivers Act, Land and Waters Conservation Fund Act, establishment of the North Cascades National Park, and the law prohibiting shooting wildlife from airplanes – then you have the evidence of his influence, character and determination to assure a healthy environment for all Americans.

His first big fight, the one that propelled him into the front ranks of conservation, was the struggle of the 1950s against construction of the proposed Echo Park Dam in Dinosaur National Monument, Utah. Most Western congressmen favored the project. It marked the first serious challenge of their pet agency, the Bureau of Reclamation, and the first time that national media focused broad public attention on a seemingly regional resource issue. In 1956, after much debate, Congress eliminated Echo Park from the Colorado River Storage Project.

The crux of the matter was not simply the integrity of Echo Park, but of all national parks, wildlife refuges and other natural preserves. By midcentury the material needs of a rapidly growing population had darkened the prospects for continued existence of the wild places.

On July 12, 1956, he declared on the House floor: "We are a great people because we have been successful in developing and using our marvelous natural resources; but, also, we Americans are the people we are largely because we have had the influence of the wilderness on our lives." Those words were part of his statement introducing the Wilderness

Bill into Congress.

It was uphill all the way. At first it was impossible to get the executive branch of government to take the bill seriously. Then, after the Interior and Agriculture departments and the Bureau of the Budget submitted favorable reports, the House and Senate refused to act. The Senate did more than the House: it held hearings during two congressional sessions. The House held only short hearings during one session, but Mr. Saylor and his supporters couldn't even get the transcript printed.

He never gave up. "I cannot believe that the American people have become so crass, so dollar-minded, so exploitation-conscious that they must develop every last little bit of wilderness that still exists," Mr. Saylor declared in 1961. That was the year President John F. Kennedy urged enactment of a wilderness preservation bill. And finally it was passed in 1964, eight years after the first bill had been introduced.

Meanwhile, Mr. Saylor helped to establish the Outdoor Recreation Resources Review Commission in 1958 and served as a commission member. From this effort emerged the Land and Water Conservation Fund, a program that gave him great pride. The Fund has been virtually the sole source of land acquisition money for national parks, forests, recreation areas and seashores. But it also has been a major stimulant to state, local and regional governments to expand their recreation programs.

Then he served on the Public Land Law Review Commission, a minority influence aboard a highly questionable craft created by Congress at the behest of his chronic adversary, Representative Aspinall. The PLLRC consumed seven million dollars of public funds and five years of study and research, involving nineteen commission members, forty-eight staff members, twenty-five advisory council members, representatives of fifty governors, six paid consultants, and nine hundred public witnesses.

After the report of the commission had been made public, Mr. Saylor delivered a speech in 1971 in which he gave his own evaluation. The membership, he said, had been stacked, weighted and loaded. "There was hardly an all-out conservationist in the whole lot. On important environmental issues, I often felt that I was standing entirely alone. Outclassed, outnumbered and outgunned, the national conservation and environmental problems inherent in the study by the commission were neatly smothered, ignored, or shunted below the dominant-use philosophy which characterized the approach of the commission's membership."

He would often express himself in such colorful language. Here are a few samples on key resource issues, excerpted from statements on the

House floor, speeches before conservation groups, or other published documents:

On the Mining Act of 1872: "The Constitution of the United States is nearly two hundred years old and it is still a sound, workable document. The mining law is nearly one hundred years old and it is an abomination and insult to the people of the United States."

On timber: "The Congress, in refusing to debate the infamous Timber Supply Act, maintained our national policy of protecting the public forests from the ravages of the timber-cutting industry. The effect of President Nixon's 'directions' to the Agriculture, Housing, and Interior secretaries was to do by executive fiat what could not be done legislatively... Conservation, environment, ecology – that is, the public's concerns – are to be subservient to the pressures of the logging and lumber industry."

On the Alaska pipeline: "Why the rush? This oil has been in the ground for a billion years. It has been discovered in the last twenty-four months. Because a few companies have invested a lot of money is no reason to lay down and play dead."

On grazing: "These bills [sponsored by former Representative Aspinall and former Senator Gordon Allot, both of Colorado] seek to give a twenty-year renewable right to graze the public lands with little or no limitation placed on how the grazing would be performed. Under the Aspinall-Allot proposals, ranching would be compensated for any reduction in grazing privileges. This is the antithesis of the free-roaming cowboy, western, frontier spirit. It is the guaranteed-income plan for stockmen."

On predator control: "The war on predators has been waged with little scientific knowledge of their beneficial roles, or with little moral or ethical consideration for man's responsibility in conserving natural life as an integral part of the environment. The operations of one division of the Bureau of Sport Fisheries and Wildlife [later the Fish and Wildlife Service], sanctioned and sheltered by one administration after another, are sinister and contemptible. Yet it continues unleashed and virtually unchallenged."

Mr. Saylor had hoped, with the advent of a Republican administration, to be named Secretary of the Interior. It would have been the culmination of his public career. Certainly he had the background and qualifications to make an outstanding Secretary in the Age of the Environment. He was too independent, too committed to the public interest to be included in an administration marked by conformity, indecision, political expediency, and liaison with the special economic interests. If Walter Hickel lasted twenty-two months, it is hardly likely that John Saylor would have lasted out the first year.

Nevertheless, his name will be remembered long after those in executive policy positions are gone and forgotten. He left his mark on Congress and on natural resource policy as did few men of his time. He takes his place in history alongside Gifford Pinchot, another Pennsylvanian, and Theodore Roosevelt as Republican leaders who blazed conservation trails.

John Saylor was not a liberal in all things. He may have received the John Muir Medal from the Sierra Club, but he also received the distinguished service award from the ultra-conservative Americans for Constitutional Action. This underscores a point I have made repeatedly: conservation belongs to no party and to no single point of view. Conservation is open territory, with plenty of room for all.

Representative Saylor gave a new dimension to the politics of conservation. He was a prophet in his own time, one of the few men in Washington who foresaw the inevitable onrushing environmental crisis, the need to husband our diminishing stock of natural resources.

My personal appraisal is that he was motivated by good old-fashioned American patriotism. He was deeply involved, for example, in efforts to save the landscape in and around Washington, He saw the capital area as a shrine of the nation, a model to display before the world. A few years ago he helped block the Democrats in power from the marshes on the Virginia side of the Potomac River below Washington, which they thought should be filled in for high-rise development. More recently he helped stop the Republicans from giving away the federal interest in the waterfront of historic Alexandria, George Washington's hometown. He was the prime mover in Congress in the establishment of Piscataway Park, embracing seven miles of the Potomac River on the Maryland shore of the Potomac River in order to preserve the vista from George Washington's mansion at Mount Vernon.

The loss of such a leading figure is always a tragic blow, yet compensated by the legacy and lessons he leaves behind. John Saylor rowed upstream against the Watergate tide. He showed that politics could be used for good purpose. Democracy, like the use of the outdoors, is not simply a right but a responsibility. The best tribute outdoorsmen can pay to the memory of this fallen friend is to become involved, participating at some stage of life in some form of the political process. Alas, we no longer can say, "Let Big John do it."

Field & Stream, 1974.

12. Only the individualist succeeds

My evaluation of the effectiveness and importance of interpretation begins and ends with the interpreter. Real success or failure, after all, comes only from within. Society, or even the best of institutions, cannot impose it from without. With all credit to the traditions and creed of the National Park Service, only the individualist succeeds, for only self-realization is success.

Joseph Wood Krutch, author, critic, and lover of nature, enunciated principles of individual rights and individual dignity. He considered America's problems basically philosophical and spiritual and felt that we must find the answers inside ourselves before looking for a political solution. I myself believe that both processes should be concurrent, but I respect Krutch and would not want to make him over. His writing was moving and powerful; he championed individual freedom and the right of self-expression.

Krutch observed and was distressed by the degradation of the southwest desert and by the galloping urbanization of Tucson, where he lived his last years, but an urge to do something about it in an organized way lay beyond him. The closest he came to activism was in his involvement in the Arizona-Sonora Desert Museum, where he shared the efforts of Arthur N. Pack and William H. Carr to display and interpret desert animals in conditions similar to their native environment.

I appreciate the role of such facilities, with their professional naturalists at work, yet I lament their studied avoidance of critical issues across the fence. Or, as the director of the Palm Springs Desert Museum – a classy oasis filled with lovely natural science exhibits, yet surrounded by a deteriorating and polluted environment – told me in 1978: "Our board doesn't want us to be involved."

Justice William O. Douglas was subject to more powerful pressures than any museum director or park interpreter. His detractors detested his far-ranging activism. Why, they demanded, couldn't he exercise judicial restraint and propriety? He brushed them off, unbending: "A man or woman who becomes a justice should try to stay alive; a lifetime diet of the law turns most judges into dull, dry husks." (Which recalls John Muir's warning that "dry words and dry facts will not fire hearts." He commented further, "In drying plants, botanists often dry themselves.")

William O. Douglas followed his own star. On January 20, 1980, shortly after his death, the *Washington Post* paid him editorial tribute:

"Whether sitting on the bench of the Supreme Court, where he served longer than any other justice in history, or before a campfire in a desolate wilderness, he knew what he believed and what he wanted."

In 1972 Justice Douglas issued his historic dissent in the Mineral King case (Sierra Club vs. Morton). The immediate question at hand was whether the Sierra Club merited legal standing to be heard in court. The majority ruled against it, but Justice Douglas in his dissent noted that a corporation or even a ship, an inanimate object, could achieve standing in the adjudicatory process. Then he continued:

> So it should be as respects valleys, alpine meadows, rivers, lakes, estuaries, beaches, ridges, groves of trees, swampland, or even air that feels the destructive pressures of modern technology and modern life. The river, for example, is the living symbol of all the life it sustains or nourishes - fish, aquatic insects, water ouzels, otter, fishers, deer, elk, bear, and all other animals, including man, who are dependent on it or who enjoy it for its sight, its sound, or its life. The river as plaintiff speaks for the ecological unit of life that is part of it. Those people who have a meaningful relation to that body of water - whether it be a fisherman, a canoeist, a zoologist, or a logger - must be able to speak for the values which the river represents and which are threatened with destruction.

Justice Douglas failed to include interpreters in his list - understandably given the context of his statement - but I certainly would include them in my list. My evaluation of effectiveness and importance furthermore equates the individual interpreter to his or her meaningful relation to the river and all other bodies of nature and the extent to which he or she speaks actively for values threatened with destruction.

It isn't enough to view national parks, as Enos Mills did, as "the school of nature." It isn't even enough to accept Freeman Tilden's uplifting idea, as expressed in *Interpreting Our Heritage*:

Thousands of naturalists, historians, archeologists and other specialists are engaged in the work of revealing, to such visitors as desire the service, something of the beauty and wonder, the inspiration and spiritual meaning that lie behind what the visitor can with his senses perceive. This function of the custodians of our treasures is called Interpretation.

That part of it is easy. The interpreter's greater challenge is to contribute consciously and conscientiously to making reserves – parks, forests, wildlife refuges, or whatever – into genuine demonstration models of ecological harmony imparting to visitors an understanding of the natural life-support system; and, no less important, taking the message of the reserves from the actual setting to the people where they live.

"The biggest problem has been, and will continue to be, convincing the public of the need for sound management, protection, and preservation," Russell E. Dickenson told me soon after he became director of the National Park Service. "If we fail to make Americans aware of problems facing the national parks, and to involve them in choosing the right solutions to these problems, then we are failing in our responsibility as stewards of these public resources."

In this same vein, a lesson I learned from Horace M. Albright years ago is that the act of establishing a national park is not enough in itself to make it work. National parks, national forests, national wildlife refuges, state parks, state forests, county and city parks – not a single tract of public land has its future assured simply with a label, or with a staff of paid professionals, or with highly motivated interpreters pointing out the beauty and wonder of nature. What is most needed, as Horace expressed it, is "wider support from more citizens who will take the trouble to inform themselves of new needs and weak spots in our conservation program."

William H. Ehorn, superintendent of Channel Islands National Park, before a conference on national parks research at Davis, California, in September, 1984, echoed this idea:

> The public needs to be constantly and consistently dealt with and consulted about the purpose and importance of our national parks. An excellent public relations program is necessary to sell the park and its management programs. This needs to be done on all levels (local, regional, state, national, and international). Once the public becomes aware and understands our mission, it becomes easier to accomplish our research and resource management objectives.

Yet national parks cannot be uncoupled from the world around them. They cannot endure as valid ecological sources of inspiration and spiritual meaning in surroundings of worsening environmental decay. They may last as national playgrounds and flawed memorials to times past, with interpreters valiantly trying to communicate with huge crowds scarcely aware of what might have been; but the preservation essence will diminish until it disappears in a period not far off.

Human restraints and a change in direction of society are essential to the survival of nature reserves. Too many people are visiting the national parks at the same time. Because they are unprepared for their experience, they do the wrong things, damaging the resource and failing to derive the vital lessons that nature has to teach.

I recall the surge of interpretation in national parks during the early 1950s. People were flocking to the parks in the post-World War II travel boom, and these people had to be cared for. Along with old guided walks and campfire talks there would be visitor centers. Instead of a naturalist out on the trail with a handful of people, an interpreter at the visitor center could process ten times or a hundred times as many. There was little talk about limiting the number of visitors to the carrying capacity of an area, or about taking the message of the parks out of the parks so that Americans would understand why they must not overrun them. It seemed too much to expect that people would actually prepare themselves for entering into the hallowed places, but interpretation became the means of a quick fix.

What we need today is a revolution of thought to challenge and revamp old institutions: medicine, religion, economics, education, science, communications, and natural resource management. Today's conditions demand a critical examination of established ideas and ideals, of old national goals and traditional personal goals measured in materialistic terms, alongside new social standards based on humanitarianism and naturalism.

Nuclear weapons will never force nations to join in recognizing the limitations of a fragile earth. But park interpreters are uniquely qualified to lead in pledging allegiance to a green and peaceful planet, based on the concept of husbanding and sharing resources, instead of allowing them to be cornered and squandered through superconsumerism and waste. In altering the lifestyle that makes us enemies of ourselves we sacrifice nothing; we gain everything in quality of life.

I know parks people, interpreters and others, who feel this way. But their opportunities for expression and leadership are circumscribed by institutional "team-play," premised on a rule that the higher up the ladder a player advances the more political, cautious, and less natural he or she becomes. Preservation of status becomes more important than preservation of resource.

In 1983 I shared an interesting exchange of correspondence with Director Dickenson. I wrote to him in part as follows:

"I wonder with apprehension about the old spark that made the National Park Service such a great institution. I can tell through personal encounters that many in the ranks have allowed themselves to be frightened and intimidated. They consider old friends and defenders of the parks almost as enemies – because we must insist on preservation principle above compromise and expediency." The director responded thoughtfully:

> Those of us who are public employees will always have to be mindful of the tug of conscience and adherence to principle vs. confrontational declarations. There are ways in which interpreters, as public servants, can inform the public of park protection issues and options, without the need for figuratively falling on one's sword, and we shall try to continue to get that message across. But, if at long last, some outrageous proposal or situation requires it, there is the honorable course of open dissent and departure. I simply take the position that talented people should not accept it lightly. Many conservation heroes and heroines undoubtedly will always arise outside the public service, and that ultimately may be the best justification in attempting to energize today's and tomorrow's park interpreters.

That sounds fair and reasonable, but whether it's right is something else. On second reading, it seems to me to demean public service. A public employee under our system, after all, works for the people under law. That is where his or her loyalty rightly belongs, which is why the Code of Ethics for Government Service opens with a declaration that: "Any person in government service should put loyalty to the highest moral principles and to country above loyalty to persons, party or government department."

Freedom of expression needs recognition and defense as an essential of good government. Diversity of opinion and even dissent should be allowed to circulate within an agency, as well as from without, like a danger warning. Insistence on respect for ecological values, no less than disclosure of waste and abuse, should be taken as a commitment to make government more responsive, more worthy of trust. The old system of power based on authority alone is dysfunctional, as evidenced by the widespread sense of powerlessness and the inefficiency of institutions. The idea of dominant authority may create an illusion of invulnerability, but living systems function synergistically, not in response to managerial authority. The power of open systems is in openness, interaction, and flexibility. It leads to cooperation instead of competition, to the creative use of the best everyone has to offer.

As I mentioned at the outset, real success or failure comes only from within. Freedom of the individual, with the right of self-expression, is sacred. Interpreters must have this freedom. They must feel this freedom as a need, like water or food, to sustain the spirit as well as the body.

This sensitivity doesn't come easily. It requires consistency and cultivation. Solitude is most important, to be alone with nature, unconditioned by refinements of modern life, preferably in a lonely place with time for contemplation and self-examination. That is what national parks ought to be for, and the kind of experience park interpreters ought to pursue to develop consistency with their message to visitors.

In the winter of 1982 I derived considerable guidance and direction from a visit with my friend, Sam West, then a river ranger at the Grand Canyon. Sam, I thought, was in control of his life as much as anyone can be, living simply, without craving superfluities. From partway down the trail inside the Grand Canyon, Sam one day pointed out the sacred mountains of the Navajo and Hopi peoples visible more than a hundred miles away. To one who releases the barriers of his mind and allows perceptions of spirit and sacredness to penetrate and register, life surely must take on broad dimensions.

"Once you're on the path," said Sam, "you see yourself with clarity; you become friends with yourself. You decide that material wealth isn't important. You become available to other people. Once you start tuning in to who you are, then it's much easier to relate to the elements, the powers that exist."

After fourteen years as guide and river ranger, Sam became program coordinator of the Open Center of New York. Part of his work is guiding trips to the Himalayas and the Grand Canyon, interpreting those areas in a way that helps people to feel part and partners of the universal design.

Another friend, Michael H. Brown, a psychologist, conducts wilderness vision quests that help "explore and develop valuable human resources that lie dormant in us all."

"It is time to speak openly and with a clear voice about the spiritual dimensions of our contact with the natural world," Michael declared in a paper presented to the Third Wilderness Congress in Scotland in October, 1983. "It is time to deliberately focus on and consciously work toward the constructive discovery, exploration, healing, enrichment and growth of the human spirit."

These approaches belong in interpretation and in the personal lives of interpreters. The true believer can work miracles after once developing a sound internal system. The best evaluation begins inside the interpreter, with the setting of personal standards and goals based on the idea that generations hence there will still be nature reserves reflecting a healthy human condition.

From *Interpretive Views*, Gary E. Machlis, editor, 1986.

13. Regreening the National Parks

In October 1991 I was invited to speak at the celebration of the seventy-fifth anniversary of the National Park Service held at Vail, Colorado. Before going there I leafed through my old copy of *Our National Parks*, the pioneering guidebook by Enos Mills. It was published in 1917, just one year after the momentous event we were commemorating, and two years after the establishment – largely through Mills' energetic efforts – of Rocky Mountain National Park. Mills in his guidebook described all seventeen parks then comprising the national park system and urged addition of at least twenty others. "Thus protected," he wrote, "these wildernesses will remain forever wild, forever mysterious and primeval, holding for the visitor the spell of the outdoors, exciting the spirit of exploration."

I offered this quotation to make the fundamental point that wilderness is at the heart of the national park ideal, and that the success or failure of national park policy and administration must be measured by the degree to which these wildernesses are protected to remain wild, mysterious and primeval.

Mills included in his guidebook a special chapter of tribute to his model, John Muir, who had died less than three years before, and whose memory, he wrote, would always be associated with the national parks and with nature's songs in wild gardens of the world. That tribute was fitting, for Muir and for the all the citizen crusaders for the parks. I felt myself a beneficiary of their noble work and continued as follows:

I regard each national park as a sanctuary to transform the human spirit. I feel uplifted and inspired by the places I have visited and by many of the people associated with them. I'm lucky to own a copy of the original *National Parks Portfolio*, which Stephen T. Mather and Robert Sterling Yard published in the earliest days. In the opening paragraph, Steve Mather wrote that the American public then possessed an empire of grandeur and beauty which it scarcely knew: "It owns the most inspiring playgrounds and the best equipped nature schools in the world and is serenely ignorant of the fact."

Mather set out to popularize the parks, which was right for his day. Now, however, it grieves me that Mather's empire of grandeur and beauty has been reduced to a chain of popcorn playgrounds, while the public scarcely comprehends the parks' deeper meaning or the need for support to sustain them.

Commemorating the seventy-fifth anniversary of the National Park Service by working toward that end – that is, to engender public awareness and involvement – is welcome, yet I feel deep concern: a sense of distress over critical issues that somehow get lost in anniversary tributes and symposia rhetoric. To illustrate, an article "Building on a Legacy" by James Ridenour, Director of the National Park Service, in the May/June issue of *National Parks Magazine* gave assurance that "The Park Service's founding mission remains fresh and valid." Mr. Ridenour wrote: "Let me stress that though we are making every attempt to address visitor needs, we are not neglecting the cultural and natural resources entrusted to our care."

That is not the way I see it. The founding mission no longer remains fresh or valid within the agency; consequently its personnel do indeed neglect the cultural and natural resources entrusted to them. In a recent issue of *Landscape Architecture Magazine*, the distinguished historian, Alfred Runte, addressed this point:

> Dignity, not development, is what national parks are about. Every conflict in the history of the national parks, and therefore every suggestion of those conflicts yet to come, can be traced to some compromise of the ideal that a national park first and foremost should exist for the preservation of its natural environment. The irony, to reemphasize, is how often that fundamental principle has been espoused while being simultaneously ignored.

The National Park Service, even at its best, is not in control of its own agenda. It's like a leaf blowing in the wind, its agenda driven by local commercial interests and allied politicians. But there is a lot less than the best as manifest in what I call loss of mission. I will cite for example a recent news report on military maneuvers in Acadia National Park. Even at the height of World War II, Director Newton B. Drury resisted every proposed military intrusion as a dangerous precedent. Now the military is accepted with open arms as a matter of course. To quote the chief ranger of Acadia: "As far as the park is concerned they [the Air National Guard] are testing new equipment and procedures and it is in the national interest for us to permit it."

National parks cannot be all things and still be national parks. Prudent, intelligent people must realize that unrestrained pressure is not progress. It may satisfy expediency today but will impoverish the future. I find the preservation and protection of wild nature, including vanishing species of wildlife driven to their last refuge in the national parks, not nearly as important as opening the parks for extraneous uses ranging from military maneuvers in Acadia to a juvenile detention center in the Delaware Water Gap and to sheer commercial-driven play and pleasure in most of the rest.

The heart of Yellowstone, the so-called "flagship" national park, has been reduced to an urban ghetto, complete with crime, litter, defacement and vandalism. In winter, rangers cater more to snowmobiles than to protection of wildlife. Voyageurs National Park in northern Minnesota in the grand design of nature was meant for wolves, but in its current administration snowmobiles come first – that place could easily be renamed Snowmobile National Park. In Virgin Islands National Park several years ago I saw beautiful palm trees uprooted to make way for pavement and parking, a hillside bulldozed flat so that a quiet road meant for leisurely touring could be "upgraded" into a high-speed highway. These examples are not exceptions; they are too much of the rule.

Such cases exemplify what I call "thinning of the blood." When the superintendent of Mount Rushmore rejects an appeal from the local Sierra Club chapter for an environmental impact statement covering a proposed $40 million construction project, that to me is "thinning the blood." When an associate director of the National Park Service testifies before a congressional committee in opposition to establishing a tallgrass national monument in Kansas, disregarding the long, hard years of effort to save some fragment of the vanishing tallgrass, that to me is "thinning the blood." When administrators fail to speak forcefully, if at all, about jets overflying national parks in Hawaii, Alaska, the West, and in Florida, that is "thinning the blood."

In cases where parks people do want to protect the sanctuaries in their charge, they are thwarted from above. Everyone here is aware of how two senior officials were dumped unceremoniously from key positions in charge of national forests and national parks in the Rocky Mountains. They weren't exactly fired, but summarily transferred out of the region; however, as they told a recent congressional hearing, they fell victim to political pressure from Western members of Congress and President Bush's own staff at the White House.

I believe these two career officials and cheer them for going public, as I'm sure that many good civil service professionals do too. Anyone in the Forest Service can easily understand the words of John Mumma, the deposed regional forester, in citing "undue interference and pressure by political figures" for ever larger timber harvests without regard for ecological consequences. Moreover, Secretary of Agriculture Madigan recently declared the Forest Service could do "a much better job cutting timber without interference from the courts." He called for an end to the appeals process and judicial review. I find that very scary – a signal that sound professional administration of our public lands, complete with citizen involvement and input, is in serious danger.

As for the National Park Service, Lorraine Mintzmyer, as a regional director testified in Congress that her efforts to prepare a 60-page "vision plan" for the future of the Greater Yellowstone Ecosystem were scuttled through pressure from John Sununu, the president's chief of staff, and subsequently weakened because of "strictly political concerns."

These recent unhappy events don't surprise me. The chambers of commerce in communities like Cody, Wyoming, through their congressional representatives exercise virtual veto power in the administration of Yellowstone National Park. That is almost standard throughout the system, explaining why the wildest, most remote areas are badly degraded. Unless the old park service takes control again, sharing full partnership with knowledgeable caring citizenry, the condition of the parks will continue downhill and politics will ruin them.

Yes, of course, the country currently is led by George Bush, a self-styled "environmental president." EPA Administrator Bill Reilly in his speech at the opening of this symposium referred to the recent rating of the president's environmental performance by a panel of experts assembled by the National Parks and Conservation Association. I was especially interested since I was the member of the panel who gave the Bush administration a D grade for "dangerous and deceitful." Bill said that "D is not a plausible grade... Don't you think an occasional carrot is in order?" Maybe so, but this morning I read a newspaper account of a press conference following his speech here at which Administrator Reilly supported oil drilling in the Arctic Wildlife Refuge. That doesn't add up.

I want Mr. Bush to succeed as an environmental president. Possibly I should characterize his administration as disorganized rather than as deceitful. He fishes, hunts, and at opportune moments drops in at Mount Rushmore and the Grand Canyon for photo opportunities, but let's face it, his energy plan, his highway plan, his moves to undermine the protection of wetlands and of the spotted owl in the Northwest, and virtually all of his appointments to key positions show George Bush as an anti-environmental Ronald Reagan rerun. D is the fair and fitting grade.

This does not fully explain the plight of the national parks and National Park Service. Politics and political meddling are not new. A review of history will show the difference between then and now. Early park leaders worked closely with concerned Americans; they recognized the citizen role.

> Each one of these national parks in America is the result of some great man's thought of service to his fellow citizens. These parks did not just happen; they came about because earnest men and women became violently excited at the possibility of these great assets passing from public control.

So declared J. Horace McFarland in testifying before a congressional committee in 1916. He might have had in mind Enos A. Mills, the father of Rocky Mountain National Park, but there were many others elsewhere as well. McFarland himself, as president of the American Civic Association, did his share and more by pressing for legislation to establish a new agency to administer the parks. And since his time, were it not for caring citizens, combining hope with activism, the Colorado River would be dammed where it runs through the Grand Canyon, the great forests would be long gone from the Olympic Peninsula and through the logging mills, the Great Smoky Mountains would be uglified with a transmountain highway, the Everglades would be bordered by a massive jetport, and Civil War battlefields covered with shopping malls and subdivisions.

To my mind, recapturing the cooperative spirit of the park pioneers should be a prime objective of this seventy-fifth anniversary. But the National Park Service is too weak, worn and weary to spread the message. Institutions generally, by their nature, tend to breed conformity and compliance. The larger and older the institution the less vision it expresses or tolerates. Surely that explains at least in part the collapse of Soviet communism in Europe. That system failed because it had no checks or balances, no tolerance for differing views, let alone dissent; it suffered institutional inbreeding, denying the means to renew itself. Any system based on deceit and ruled by force only erodes trust, effectiveness and leadership. It destroys initiative, programming people to conform, to adapt their personalities and goals to established standards of society, rather than to cultivate their own potential or to challenge society, and thus contribute to its enrichment.

The National Park Service is no exception to the rule. Its personnel may voice concern for ecology as a principle, but scarcely as something specific in critical need of defense. The best defense is an alert and alarmed public, but national parks personnel are generally inward oriented. They know the public as visitor numbers, but not as decision-makers. The parks person is a professional, which is how he or she learned to appreciate the values of ecology in principle, but conformity and compromise in practice.

Yes, able, wilderness-conscious, ecosystem-conscious people are at work, but they often do their best against heavy odds. They are frustrated and unfulfilled preparing policy statements, manuals, plans and promises proclaiming the future of wilderness, which they recognize as mostly bureaucratic paperwork. Good people in the ranks want to do more; they deserve a better break.

A national park as I see it is not simply a place. It's an ideal, a mission, an old mystique that sets national parks and park people apart, a mystique yearning for rebirth. The seventy-fifth anniversary provides a marvelous opportunity to recharge old batteries. Let us go on from this conference to rescue everything that still remains wild and to recapture a lot more that has been lost. Let us not privatize the parks with the goodies of Disneyesque "partnerships" and the strings attached to them. There are no enemies. The children of the poor will become rich for what is saved; the children of the rich will be impoverished for what may be lost.

No other country is so enriched by its parks, forests, wildlife refuges and other reserves administered by towns, cities, counties, states and the federal government. Those areas must be models of land stewardship. Let the National Park Service and those who care take the lead, advancing love of the beautiful as a principle of patriotism so that life may be more elevating and Americans may love their country more the more lovable it is made.

It takes considerable courage to work through the system, but it's the best system we have. "New opinions are always suspected, and usually opposed," wrote John Locke, "without any other reason but because they are not already common." Such is the way of institutions, but not of individuals. Each individual must realize the power of his or her own life and never sell it short; the great use of a life is to create something that outlasts it. With vision, caring, courage and hope, park pioneers turned dreams into reality. The great lesson of this anniversary commemoration is that we now can do the same – that we can regreen the national parks.

From remarks at Commemoration of the 75th Anniversary
of the National Park Service, Vail, Colorado, 1991

14. A wilderness original:
Bob Marshall

"His eyes reflected a great joy for living." Paul Schaefer observed after first meeting Robert Marshall on a climb in the Adirondack Mountains in 1932. Those few words in a sense tell it all, for Bob Marshall, a truly major figure in the unfolding history of conservation, packed joy and life into his years. The years, alas, were all too few, his life all too short.

Bob Marshall died unexpectedly in 1939 at the age of thirty-eight, yet he left a rich legacy of inspiration and challenge. Starting with boyhood summers in upstate New York, he explored wild places across the country and in Alaska, but he made clear that using wilderness, even for recreation, is not enough. One must give for wilderness as well as take from it. In his case, as a professional forester and federal official, Marshall debated and influenced public policy – I daresay there would be no National Wilderness Preservation System today without his pioneering efforts and ideas. Moreover, he called on wilderness lovers to join together to defend and advance the wilderness cause. And that is what we need to do today, more than ever.

The life of the "wilderness original" makes great reading, but it also provides his original rationale for saving special places everywhere. For example, to arguments that wilderness designation "locks up" and withholds resources from public use, Marshall responded that a truly democratic society proves itself with respect for the rights of the few. When asked by critics how much wilderness it would take to satisfy him, he replied, "How many Brahms symphonies do we need?"

I read and enjoyed James Glover's biography of Bob Marshall when it was first published by The Mountaineers in 1986. Reading it anew I recognize and appreciate dimensions beyond his concern for wilderness that made Marshall a whole person. From his father, a famed constitutional lawyer and international Jewish leader, he inherited a sense of human rights and human dignity. Thus Marshall supported progressive causes – civil liberties, peace, social justice – along with conservation. That makes sense to me, for surely natural and human environments are indivisible.

The book tells of his gifted family and his friends, including Herb Clark and Paul Schaefer, stalwarts of the Adirondacks; Harvey Broome, Bernard Frank and Benton MacKaye, with whom he divined a new organization, the Wilderness Society; and Gifford Pinchot, his ally in socially conscious forestry. He was blessed with friends at many different stations in society, and American society is blessed that Robert Marshall, all too briefly, came its way.

"The world has lost a great humanitarian," wrote his colleague John Sieker, "and the Forest Service has lost a conservationist who was willing and able to fight for the principles of true conservation to the end." Still, I hope that a new generation will discover him and follow his call.

Foreword to *A Wilderness Original – The Life of Robert Marshall*,
by James Glover, 1996.

15. "Earth man":
Harvey Broome

Harvey Broome, a gifted man of the law, was also in the forefront when it came to ecology. In hiking, backpacking, and camping he was a joyous companion. When it came to the preservation of the unique wildness which this continent once knew, he was advocate extraordinary. And when it came to writing about the outdoors and the wilderness, I always rated him along with Henry Thoreau and John Muir.
– William O. Douglas, 1972

To those words of Justice Douglas I say, Amen!

And again, Amen to the words of Senator Howard Baker, of Tennessee, who declared in tribute, soon after Harvey's death in 1968: "Mr. Broome's love of nature was the hallmark of his life. America has lost a great citizen."

Harvey would be embarrassed by such words of praise, for he was modest to a fault. But few Americans, in any era, ever achieved his special relationship with the out-of-doors. His close friend Benton MacKaye called him "Earth Man," and that he was. He honored the earth and knew it intimately in all seasons. But he generously shared his earth-love. As president of the Wilderness Society, an organization that he helped found, for example, Harvey was an able, inspiring spokesman for a movement that has penetrated deep into the conscience of America. That was one way he shared.

He traveled widely across the continent and recorded his explorations for us to read and appreciate, and that was another way. Starting in 1928, Harvey kept journals covering all his hikes in the Smokies and beyond. He edited the annual handbook of the Smoky Mountains Hiking Club, which itself constitutes exceptional nature writing. Later, his friend Howard Zahniser, executive director of the Wilderness Society, invited Harvey to contribute a series of "Mountain Notebooks" to *The Living Wilderness*, the quarterly journal of the Society, which Zahniser edited.

Following his death, Anne Broome, Harvey's wife, felt inspired to assemble and publish his work in book form. They were the closest of companions and she felt it her happy fortune to share his life and work. Anne consulted Paul Oehser, who served with Harvey on the governing council (board of directors) of the Wilderness Society and had long been in charge of publications at the Smithsonian Institution in Washington. With Oehser's encouragement and guidance, *Harvey Broome: Earth Man*, a collection of miscellaneous essays, was published in 1970. This was followed two years later by *Faces of the Wilderness*, a collection of largely personal accounts of field trips taken by the council of the Wilderness Society in conjunction with its annual meetings, from its first in 1946 up through 1965. Through those pages, the reader became privy to discoveries, discomforts and exhilarations of wilderness travel in various sections of the country, on seashores, in deserts, and high in the mountains, from Alaska to the Everglades.

And then in 1975 came *Out Under the Sky of the Great Smokies: A Personal Journal*, a substantial volume illustrated with line drawings by Larry Hirst. Harvey actually had worked on this book before his death. He wrote the acknowledgments and introduction as they appear in print, and the work preserves the sequence just as he envisioned it. While preparing these lines I have just picked up my cloth bound copy of the original edition. I note the inside flap presents three endorsements. One from A.J. Sharp, a distinguished botany professor at the University of Tennessee, called the book "A superb account of the recurrent joys and spiritual rejuvenation found in wilderness." Stanley A. Cain, who also taught at Tennessee before going to the University of California, Santa Cruz, wrote: "This private journal, the most intimate of writings, is part of Harvey Broome's bequest to those who love people other than themselves." And I see the third endorsement is from myself: "The focus may be on the Smokies, but Mr. Broome expresses a sense of universality that should appeal to lovers of nature the world over."

That was more than a quarter century ago, to be sure, but now, in a new generation, Kenneth Wise has advised the publisher that he has been hiking in the Smokies since he was twelve and that he has used Mr. Broome's journals as an academic research source and hiking guide. He cites the historic value of the journals as the only written accounts of old trails and paths that no longer exist. He believes that "No other writer conveys to the reader a better visual image of the Smoky Mountains wilderness. It is remarkably free of errors." As author of the contemporary popular guide *Hiking Trails in the Great Smoky Mountains*, Kenneth Wise should know.

Out Under the Sky is a timeless work. Here we find Harvey, the wilderness apostle, on his home turf. He reveals himself exactly as I knew and loved him: a gentle spirit, sensitive to the needs of nature and humankind, always with tolerance and good humor. On my first hike with him in the Great Smoky Mountains, we ventured to the Chimney Tops, a steep climb, almost vertical for several hundred feet, hand over hand from one rocky perch to the next. It was raining and I dared to complain. Harvey brushed me off with a laugh. "You don't complain about weather in the Smokies. You learn to accept it!"

Harvey saw the Smokies in every season and every mood. He was out under the skies when the temperature dropped to fifteen below zero, and the trees cracked and popped throughout the night, and the ice froze on his eyebrows and eyelashes, and the water froze in his canteen. He met and marveled at bears, snakes, and spiders, along with the more accept-able plants and trees. "Trees are very satisfying. They stay put; they don't go out at night; they don't have dates... Living less complex lives, they are not as stimulating as people, although, on the other hand, they are less dis-appointing than many people."

He began his lifelong love affair with the Smokies in another age in history. It was already the twentieth century but little changed from the nineteenth. Clusters of rural settlement like Sugarlands and Cades Cove were largely isolated from outside civilization. Mountain people lived as their parents had lived before them. They grazed cattle on the grassy balds, following old pathways. The most significant intrusions into the wild Smokies were then underway by logging outfits and their railroads, but few trails led to the inaccessible peaks.

Harvey B. (for Benjamin) Broome was born in Knoxville in 1902, when it was not yet a city, but a provincial valley town, like most of the South still in arrested development following the Civil War. People walked to work, school and church, rode the few electric trolleys, or rode bicycles, which outnumbered automobiles. As he recorded in *Out Under the Sky*, he was born at home, since there was one hospital in town and that rarely used for birthing. Harvey's father, George William Broome, had come to America as a child with his parents from Shropshire, England, in 1872. His mother's family was of early revolutionary stock. His grandfather, James Harvey Smith (on his mother's side), died at the age of ninety-two in the brick house where he was born, near the intersection of North Broadway and Tazewell Pike.

The defining moment in Harvey's life came early, when he was fifteen. Because he was slightly built and sickly, an uncle offered to take him on a camping trip in the Smokies. He came to the mountains to build his health hiking and camping, and then came again and again, in much the same way as another sickly boy, William O. Douglas (who the doctors feared would never reach maturity), camped and hiked in the Washington Cascades, and in the same way as sickly Theodore Roosevelt in the 1880s when he fled the East to the Badlands of North Dakota.

Harvey traveled from Knoxville on the Little River Railroad, an adventure in itself into logging camps and through deep water gaps. His first hike, in 1917, was to Silers Bald, his first climb to the Chimney Tops in 1920. In Knoxville, he was a good student planning a professional career, but his heart and mind were bound from the start with the Great Smoky Mountains wilderness.

Harvey was graduated from the University of Tennessee in 1923 and three years later from Harvard Law School. For all the benefits of formal education, his best learning came from two other connections that continued through the rest of his life. One was with Benton MacKaye, regional planner, philosopher and wilderness apostle, to whom Harvey dedicated *Out Under the Sky*. The other powerful lasting connection was with the Smoky Mountains Hiking Club. I'm not sure that Harvey was a member when the club was organized in 1924 – he may have been away at law school in Cambridge – but he certainly became involved in the 1920s, and remained close to it until he died.

Benton MacKaye was a New Englander, graduated from Harvard with a forestry degree in 1904 and then employed by the US Forest Service for twelve years before pioneering in regional planning and social and land reform. In 1921 he wrote an article titled "An Appalachian Trail: A Project in Regional Planning" in the *Journal of the American Institute of Architects*, which he circulated widely. The Appalachian Trail, or AT, since MacKaye's time has become a considerable recreational resource, but he saw it then and thereafter as something more: the means of making each metropolis a place of cultural individuality and unity, based on its own natural setting, "a sanctuary from the scramble of everyday worldly commercial life." He was thinking of protecting wilderness, much like his contemporaries, Arthur Carhart and Aldo Leopold. In his 1921 article, MacKaye wrote: "Wilderness is two things – fact and feeling. It is a fund of knowledge and a spring of influence. It is the ultimate source of health."

Scattered groups and individuals responded to MacKaye's proposal and within two years completed sections of the trail. Early in 1925, leaders of various clubs convened in Washington, DC, for the founding meeting of the Appalachian Trail Conference. MacKaye attended and outlined the philosophy he hoped would guide it. He wanted local initiative to count most. He felt it proper that government agencies administer the land but essential that volunteers, through the clubs, maintain and protect the

Appalachian Trail.

Following the 1925 conference, individuals and groups along the Trail did wonderful things to advance its goals. The Smoky Mountains Hiking Club assumed responsibility for the length of the Trail across the Smokies, then still wild and little known, at a time when the movement to establish a national park was just getting underway. The club aimed to increase interest in hiking and love of the mountains by disseminating information and taking beginners on hikes, initially scheduled once a month to key landmarks like Mount LeConte, the grassy balds of Thunderhead and Gregory, the Chimney Tops and the big trees in Porter's Flats. In 1927 the schedule was increased to two hikes a month throughout the year and the hiking program enlarged from a leaflet to a substantial handbook. Harvey Broome by now was corresponding secretary and editor of the handbook, and thus left us a record of his own and the club's activities.

Trip leaders in those early days (in addition to Harvey) included Jim Thompson, the photographer, whose pictures illustrated the handbook; Laura Thornburgh, author of an early guidebook to the Smokies; Ed Meeman, editor of the Knoxville *News-Sentinel* (who led a moonlight hike from Cades Cove to Gregory's Bald) and Jack Huff, whose family built and ran the Mountain View Hotel in Gatlinburg. The handbook is filled with cheery, positive writing, mostly Harvey's. In the 1929 edition he published a poem of his own titled "Winter" (signed H.B.B), which includes this stanza:

> It's the powdery snow in the moonlight,
>   A canvas for brilliance and gloom;
> It's the close, peaked ranks of the balsams,
>   Creaking and popping as at doom;
> It's the air, crisp and bitter as poison,
>   Which chills me and cuts to the bone;
> The resistless spell of dead winter,
>   That seizes and makes me her own.

Harvey returned from Harvard to pursue a successful law practice in Knoxville, first as law clerk to a judge, then in private practice. That was the professional side of life. On the personal side, he became the fifth president of the club in 1932, the year all the trails in the park were completed and when Harvey and seven others hiked the full length. It took them nine days.

He also established continuing contact with MacKaye. To show the closeness of their connection, Harvey in 1926 had met Anna (subsequently Anne) Waller Pursel, a native of Bloomsburg, Pennsylvania, at Cambridge while she worked as a secretary at the Harvard Law School. They corresponded, kept in touch and fell in love. Harvey introduced her to his friend MacKaye, who invited them to be married in the living room of his home at Shirley Center, Massachusetts; and so it took place in 1937.

MacKaye himself was married for a few years early in life and then became a lifelong bachelor, with little ambition or need for material wealth. He worked here and there as a planner and consultant, but he most enjoyed projecting his philosophy on the role of nature in regionalism. I recall visiting him in retirement at Shirley Center. He was over ninety, still cheery with new ideas. He insisted on taking me to lunch and drove his car to get there. (He died in 1976 at age 97.)

MacKaye broadened Harvey's ideas and probably influenced his writing style as well. For example, in an article on "The Appalachian Trail: A Guide to the Study of Nature," in *Scientific Monthly*, April 1932, MacKaye wrote: "Primeval influence is the opposite of machine influence. It is the antidote for over-rapid mechanization. It is getting feet on the ground with eyes toward the sky – not eyes on the ground with feet on a lever. It is feeling what you touch and seeing what you look at." On November 15, 1933 he wrote Harvey's sister, Margaret Broome (later Howes), as chairman of the Handbook Committee, in response to her request for a message of greeting for the Handbook:

> Friendship is a hard thing to define. To me it is a portion of creation held in common. Our special portion (yours and mine) we call the wilderness – the portion untarnished by act of man. Such is our common bond. To cherish it (even as human fellowship itself) – such is our common goal.
>
> For we need this thing wilderness far more than it needs us. Civilizations (like glaciers) come and go, but the mountain and its forest continue the course of creation's destiny. And in these we mere humans can take part – by fitting our civilization to the mountain.
>
> This, friend Margaret, is the thing that you are doing (you and your Clubmates) – you who have wrought your portion of the Appalachian Trail – you who cherish the Great Smoky Mountains for yourselves and all America.

In 1934 MacKaye came to Knoxville for a two-year assignment on the planning staff of the Tennessee Valley Authority. Likely he and Harvey welcomed the opportunity to work closely, but they could hardly have foreseen the momentous consequences of their collaboration.

That year, 1934, they met twice in Knoxville with Robert Marshall, a young man in his thirties who was pioneering federal programs in wilderness protection. Marshall as a boy in New York had tramped all across the Adirondacks (in the same way that Broome had tramped the Smokies) and gone on to adventurous hikes all across the continent and to a successful career in government. On this occasion he was on assignment from Secretary of the Interior Harold L. Ickes to view the effects of New Deal road building projects on the Great Smoky Mountains. After Marshall and Broome climbed Clingmans Dome, Marshall reported to Ickes in a memo (August 18, 1934):

> I hiked to Clingmans Dome last Sunday, looking forward to the great joy of undisturbed nature for which this mountain has been famous. Walking along the skyline trail, I heard instead the roar of machines on the newly constructed road just below me and saw the huge scars which this new highway is making on the mountain. Clingmans Dome and the primitive were simply ruined.

Then on another visit to Knoxville one month later, Marshall met again with MacKaye and Broome and also Bernard Frank, then a TVA forester, to conceive a new organization to be called the Wilderness Society and a few months later the society was duly constituted. From the very beginning until the end of his life, Harvey Broome was a central figure to development of the society's ideology and implementation through law and regulation.

Aldo Leopold, who had seen national forest wilderness disturbed and destroyed, joined the group. So did Olaus J. Murie, a well-respected field biologist who had conducted important studies in Alaska and Wyoming. Robert Sterling Yard, who had been journalist, editor, and early publicity chief of the National Park Service, in 1935 became the part-time executive secretary (and later president) of the society. Yard had become disillusioned with commercialization of the national parks and had dreamed of starting "an organization to preserve the primitive."

Bob Marshall, the young crusader, died in 1939 at the age of thirty-eight, and then Robert Sterling Yard, the old crusader, died in 1945 at eighty-four, but they left the wilderness movement well defined and the Wilderness Society in the hands of committed and caring colleagues. Following Yard's death, Olaus Murie became director, based in Wyoming, and Howard Zahniser, formerly a government editor, became executive secretary, based in Washington. Zahniser, or "Zahnie," I well remember from personal contact as studious, soft-spoken, patient, always willing to listen, always resisting the seduction of compromise. He drafted the Wilderness Bill in 1956, found sponsors, and worked tirelessly for its passage.

Zahniser and Broome were colleagues and comrades. Edward Zahniser, the son of Howard, remembers from childhood "Harvey's wry, affectionate smile, his attentiveness and gentleness, a strength in his love for Anne." Because their own grandfathers were dead, the four Zahniser children felt free to call Harvey "Grampa." The whole Zahniser family would visit Harvey and Anne in Knoxville and at their cabin at Cobbles Hollow, in Emerts Cove, at the edge of the national park. The cabin was built with logs, an open fireplace, kerosene lamps, its own spring, and a view down a ravine to Mount LeConte. It was a great starting place for hikes into cove hardwood forests and into the high country.

Zahniser appreciated Harvey's writing and invited him to contribute regularly to the quarterly *The Living Wilderness*, which Zahniser edited. Considering the Wilderness Society was still a small struggling organization with a few thousand members, that magazine had little circulation and was often late in publication, but it carried articles of lasting value by gifted visionaries like Aldo Leopold, Benton MacKaye, Olaus Murie and Sigurd Olson. Harvey Broome, after visiting the Big Horn Crags in Idaho in 1961, wrote in *The Living Wilderness* as follows:

> I think how precious in such an environment and under such circumstances is one human life… It is one of our problems today that our huge cities have become frightening colossi. The individual exists, for himself and a few who know him. Otherwise, he is one of a mass to be thought of in the mass and shunted about in streams of traffic, in streams of thought, and in easy academic classifications. It took this wilderness experience to etch again the importance of a single person.

In this same period William O. Douglas, associate justice of the Supreme Court, became another intimate friend and trail companion of Harvey's, in the Smokies and elsewhere. A native of Washington State, frail and sickly as a child, Douglas found strength and purpose in the outdoors. He called the Cascades home but knew the mountains of the world and considered them all sacred.

As a strong-willed civil libertarian, Douglas bucked the political or public tide when he felt need to. "We must have freedom of speech for all," he insisted, "or we will in the long run have it for none but the cringing and the craven." And at times Douglas thought little of stepping down from the bench to become involved in earthy affairs.

For example, in 1954, the *Washington Post* published an editorial favoring construction of a parkway on the towpath of the Chesapeake & Ohio Canal, intruding into a section of the Appalachian Trail in Maryland. In what became one of the most famous letters-to-the-editor, Douglas challenged the author of the *Post* editorial, Robert Estabrook, to join in hiking the 185 miles of canal towpath between Washington and Cumberland in western Maryland. Subsequently, Douglas and thirty-six others, the editor included, rode the train to Cumberland and started down the towpath parallel to the Potomac River, through rolling pastureland, mountain gaps and historic towns. The "Immortal Nine," including Bill Douglas, Harvey Broome and Olaus Murie, averaging between twenty and twenty-seven miles a day, completed the full journey in eight days, returning to Washington in cheers. It was a bit of a Gandhian protest, as Douglas called it, and it worked. The parkway plan was discarded.

During the late fifties and early sixties the battle for the Wilderness Bill wore on. It was a hard uphill campaign. Key members of the governing council wavered and had second thoughts about pushing the bill any further. Stewart M. Brandborg, Zahnhiser's close associate and later successor, well remembers: "When Zahnie was always open to endless discussion on the topic of 'What should we do next in working for the bill?' some complained that he overdid it. I recognized its value and resented deeply the tough interrogations..." It became so bad that Zahniser despaired and was ready to quit. Edward Zahniser remembers his father's anguish, but also that "Harvey Broome emerged as the council champion of keeping at it."

Zahniser saw the campaign through, but died in May 1964, five months before the Wilderness Act became law. He was the Moses denied entry to the promised land. Harvey was already president of the Society. He had been elected in 1957 and the following year had quit his law practice to work as clerk for a federal judge in Knoxville, with the understanding that he could take reasonable time as needed to labor in behalf of the Society. Brandborg recalls as follows:

> I consulted with Harvey as a source of mentoring. He always shared in his generous, loyal way in my tribulations. Harvey usually would arrive in Washington on Friday nights for the three quarterly meetings of the executive committee on Saturdays. As a rule, he stayed with us on Saturday nights and we hiked on Sugar Loaf Mountain or the C&O Canal on Sundays until his afternoon plane for Knoxville. The kids went along and were pleased with his humor and observations on the woods and its critters.
>
> "At no time in that period from 1964 until his death do I remember a single unpleasant occasion while working closely with Harvey. It was always a matter of reasonable discussion, gentle persuasion and presentation of alternative lines of action, but never an argument. It was terribly

important to me as a young guy feeling my way that he was unfailingly willing to share his wisdom and guidance.

In 1966 Harvey lived his finest hours, the summation of a life devoted to the cause the Great Smoky Mountains and to wilderness everywhere. In that year the National Park Service announced its first wilderness proposal under terms of the Act of 1964. The agency chose for its precedent the Great Smokies, of all places, but its proposal could not have been worse. It was, in fact, an anti-wilderness proposal. As the *New York Times* editorialized June 14,1966, on the eve of public hearings:

> The Park Service has come up with a meager, unsatisfactory and essentially bureaucratic proposal that six different areas covering less than half the park be held inviolate as wilderness. It is the Park Service, supposedly the prime protector, that has plans to destroy major parts of the Smokies wilderness by constructing several highways....

The anti-wilderness design was the personal concoction of George B. Hartzog, Jr., the crafty director of the National Park Service, who had made a commitment to local North Carolina politicians for commercial-boosting highways across the Smokies and who resisted wilderness designation everywhere. "The Hartzog proposal for Great Smoky Mountains National Park was fortuitous in a way," Stewart Brandborg recalls. "It stirred Harvey's deepest emotions. We began a day-by-day strategizing process, with Harvey 'feeling the pain' of each Hartzog ploy for destroying the Great Smokies wilderness and wilderness of the entire national park system. I was green in facing this challenge and the ultimate confrontation with George and all his political chicanery, but with Harvey's thoughtful, gentle counsel we chose and steered the right course."

Harvey may have been gentle, but he was resolute as well. I saw that at close hand during this period. For three years I had been working on *Strangers in High Places*, my book about the Great Smokies, and had benefited from Harvey's experience and friendship. He took me out on the trails and into his home. Now I saw him as tough and tenacious, never once countenancing the possibility of defeat on the issues of principle.

He and his closest comrade-in-arms, Ernie Dickerman, were disciplined and determined. They gave the spark that fueled the fight. Harvey was like commander-in-chief and Dickerman the chief of staff in charge of mobilizing grassroots support in defense of the Smokies wilderness. They were old Knoxville buddies, long active in the Smoky Mountains Hiking Club. *Out Under the Sky* includes reference to many trips they made together. These range from early 1941, when they hiked to Wooly Tops, plunging into "the dead of winter, with great snow blankets, gray-green ice falls, and time-covered trees" to the historic "Save-Our-Smokies" hike on Sunday, October 23, 1966. On that day a total of 576 people walked some portion of the route from Clingmans Dome parking area out along the Appalachian Trail to Buckeye Gap, where the proposed road was intended to cross the crest of the Smokies, and then down to the Elkmont Campground. A total of 234 persons walked the entire 17 miles, the last completing the trip by moonlight.

"It is amazing how many persons from all over the country supported wilderness designation in the Great Smoky Mountains." Dickerman wrote to me in retrospect years later, "and opposed any new roads in the course of the campaign which lasted six years until George Hartzog finally threw in the towel." Or, as Stewart Brandborg recalls: "Victory in the Smokies gave us a precedent and the confidence and experience to face down the bureaucracies which continued in its opposition to wilderness designation. Harvey gave the leadership on focusing on mobilization of grassroots people who would carry the wilderness designation for lands in their states."

Following Harvey's death in 1968, Dickerman carried on. He organized a trip to Washington of almost 100 conservationists from North Carolina and Tennessee on June 23, 1969. Hartzog's political sponsor and superior at the Interior Department, Stewart L. Udall, was now gone as secretary, and the delegation called on the new secretary, Walter J. Hickel, who met with them and shook each person by the hand. "I am impressed by your numbers and sincerity of your purpose." Hickel declared. Then he humbled Hartzog by directing him and his agency to come up with a new and better plan. The transmountain road idea died there.

Dickerman was part of Harvey's circle of loyal, gifted and giving people. A lifelong bachelor, Dickerman lived simply and carried little baggage. During the campaign in the Smokies he joined the professional staff of the Wilderness Society, training and mobilizing grassroots activists, continuing on his own even after retirement in 1976. In 1986 the hiking club presented him the Harvey Broome Distinguished Service Award. He died in 1998 at age 88.

I felt privileged to be included in Harvey's circle. Staying in the house with him and Anne on Mountain Crest Drive was always uplifting and enlightening. Brick and timbers in the house had been moved to the site when the old family homestead was razed. A little of the front yard was mowed along the walkway, but the rest was strictly *au naturel* wooded and shrubby. Harvey and Anne were focused on wilderness, but had a breadth of interests. She was a weaver, with a loom in the house, doing something creative with the hands. He was a local historian, president of the East

Tennessee Historical Society from 1945 to 1947 and author of four chapters in *The French Broad-Holston Country, A History of Knox County*. Anne's parents had died when she was a child so Harvey's family became her family and one of his nieces, sister Margaret's daughter, is named Anne Broome Howes.

I saw Harvey for the last time early in 1968, a matter of weeks before he died. A few months earlier he had climbed Mt. Katahdin in Maine. Then, near Thanksgiving, he learned that he had a heart ailment. Still, he came to Washington on Wilderness Society business and had dinner with a small group of friends. While walking with him back to his hotel I saw that he looked pale and weak. The once tireless hiker felt he must stop to rest every few steps.

On Friday, March 8, 1968, Harvey collapsed and died in his yard while sawing a segment of a little hollow log to make into a wren's house. Several days later eight or ten of Harvey's intimates gathered for a service in the study of his home on Mountain Crest Drive. I remember Anne Broome, Alice Zahniser (Howard's widow), Stewart Brandborg, Ernie Dickerman, Ernest Griffiths, Michael Nadel, and Paul Oehser. Anne read selections from Harvey's journals, including this entry from April 23, 1950 about a climb in the Ramsay-Buck Fork country, at the Chapman Prong confluence with the Ramsay:

> In the deepness of twilight, we noted an elusive fragrance, and I was reminded of the fragrance which Thoreau noted several times over the course of years and which was to him so sweet and captivating that he was almost afraid to trace it to its source. He never did. We, however, followed ours to an oasis of phacelia which flanked the trail like snow – acres of it. And the heavy, tense, strenuous day came slowly, evenly, peacefully to an end, like the subsiding notes of a great symphony.

Each took a turn to express some special reminiscence. When my turn came I stared at Harvey's boots perched on a filing cabinet. I wanted to make some reference to them but felt inadequate and words stuck in my throat.

Then we drove to the park to hike to Harvey's favorite area in the section called Greenbrier. It was raining in the Smokies, a steady, drippy downpour that turned the forest misty, mellow and a little mournful. I hadn't realized what was coming and wasn't prepared for it. Anne removed from her backpack a container about the size of a Mason jar. It held Harvey's cremated remains, looking like ground chalk – all there is to any of us in the end, and no mausoleum, no matter how majestic, can make more of it. While we stood silent and thoughtful in the rain, Anne scattered the ashes. It was time to leave, but no one seemed ready or able to lead. Ernest Griffith, treasurer of the Wilderness Society, an old scholar who had already lived a full life, broke the silence. "This is a time of thanksgiving, not of mourning," he began a brief impromptu eulogy that brightened the mood. He called it a day of triumph, gratitude and dedication, and so it became.

A few days later in Washington, Representative John P. Saylor paid tribute to Harvey, as I mentioned earlier. He said that he was proud to consider himself a fellow to Bob Marshall, Olaus Murie, Howard Zahniser, and Harvey Broome: "They were all great leaders for the saving of wilderness for our time, for all time. They have passed on, but their legacy falls to new leaders, as their spirit lives on."

They have gone to their reward, John Saylor included. Anne Broome died in 1983. Of those at the service, only Alice Zahniser, Stewart Brandborg and I remain in the twenty-first century, but the spirit of them all lives on. Paul Oehser was a considerable poet and from one of his pieces, called "Song," I will conclude with these appropriate two verses.

> Let songs be crystal clear
> From countless throats, till stars shall hear
> The unyielding notes;
>
> Till songless men shall share
> The echoes coming, each unaware
> Of his own humming.

Foreword to *Out Under the Sky of the Great Smokies*, 2001.

16. Bitterrooter: Stewart M. Brandborg

In my years covering the environmental scene in Washington, D.C., from the late 1950s until the early 1980s, I knocked on many doors in Congress, government bureaus and diverse interests around town. I went frequently to the environmental organizations, large and small, militant and mild, and met and knew, to one degree or another, all of the environmental leaders of that period.

My best source, and my best mentor, was Stewart Brandborg, executive director of the Wilderness Society. He answered many, many questions, and was patient, with good humor, in contrast with some others who I found absorbed with self-importance, snobbery and jealousy of their peers. I have never, to this day, fathomed mean-spirit among people presumably working toward common goals. With Brandborg, however, I observed that both his door and heart were open. He allowed a lot of time for a lot of people, of all different kinds, whether from the *New York Times* or a local citizen group from Idaho or Iowa.

I liked the way he would not quit and eschewed compromise. In the mid-sixties, when I became interested in citizen efforts to save the Little Tennessee River from being obliterated by the Tellico Dam, I went to see the conservation director of the National Wildlife Federation. "Oh, sure," he said. "We wrote a letter." And that was the whole campaign. With Brandborg it was all-out action, whether the cause had a chance or not – and, after all, who can foretell the ultimate consequence to hearty determined effort?

For Brandborg the Wilderness Act of 1964 opened the way to a new level of citizen involvement and activism, a grassroots conservation movement in which local people could be heard in behalf of wilderness areas they know best. He seized a provision of the act stipulating that, prior to action by Congress, public hearings must be held with advance notice on each proposed new wilderness unit in the vicinity of the lands in question.

In the Spring-Summer issue of *The Living Wilderness* 1964 (No. 86), which actually appeared in the fall following passage and signing of the Wilderness Act, Brandborg wrote:

> In bringing these wild land areas into the Wilderness System the basic need will be public support. This can develop only with studies of each area by conservation groups at local and state levels in cooperation with the agencies responsible for administering the areas. Field reconnaissance coverage will be necessary for the definition of boundary proposals and development of protection programs that meet the wilderness preservation needs of each area. Following the completion of the recommendations from these studies an educational job must be done, both within the local communities and states, and on a broad national scale.

Consequently the late 1960s and early 70s were exciting times, a marvelous moment in conservation history. The early training programs of the Wilderness Society, which Brandborg initiated, were great exercises, popular and productive with the grassroots groups. Harry Crandell, who worked for the Wilderness Society from 1970 to 1975, wrote about this period: "The Society was in the forefront and led major wilderness and public land issues. We all worked together as a team, each helping the other. Successful conclusion of issues would have been highly unlikely absent citizen involvement and telephone 'trees' manned by volunteers and 'alerts' prepared by staff."

Brandborg was meant for this work. He was born and raised on the Idaho-Montana wilderness frontier. His father, Guy M.(or G.M.) Brandborg, was a two-fisted populist, who joined the Forest Service in 1914 at the age of twenty-one, committing himself through forty years in the Forest Service and retirement thereafter to leaving the earth and its resources in better condition than he found them. For twenty years as supervisor of the Bitterroot National Forest, he wrote a record of stewardship. After he retired, the Forest Service hierarchy became the victim of its love affair with clearcutting and made G.M. Brandborg's old forest the first and worst example. He fought it tooth-and-toenail, with encouragement from old friends on the inside, until he died in 1977.

In the meantime, the younger Brandborg was graduated from the University of Montana and earned a master's degree in wildlife science at the University of Idaho while conducting pioneering studies of mountain goats, principally in the Selway-Bitterroot Wilderness. Following his interests, he came to Washington in 1954 to work in the conservation department of the National Wildlife Federation. Two years later he was elected to the Wilderness Society Council (the board of directors) and in 1960 joined the Wilderness Society staff.

Howard Zahniser was his boss, teacher and best friend. "Zahnie" was the exemplar of patience, principle and courage, who had drafted the original Wilderness Bill in 1956 and kept pursuing the cause through eighteen congressional hearings over a period of eight years. He was the hero but passed on before the victory. An editorial by Edward J. Meeman in the *Memphis Press-Scimitar* of August 22, 1964 paid him tribute with the last paragraph as follows:

> Like Moses, Howard Zahniser, executive director of the Wilderness Society, who died fighting for the cause, was not here to enter the promised land of wilderness preserved. We wish he could have seen how we answered his plea that we project the wild that has come to us from the eternity of the past into the eternity of the future.

Brandborg was by all odds the logical successor, facing a new challenge to make the National Wilderness Preservation System a reality under terms of the law. He recognized the time and place for compromise, but felt also that paper victories create illusions rather than progress. I recall that a friend of mine, Roger Allin, superintendent of Olympic National Park in Washington State, in the early 1970s was assigned by his superiors to prepare a wilderness proposal for his park. The regional director advised him to omit two politically controversial portions. "Then," said the director, "we should have no difficulty in getting it through Congress." Allin refused. "I was more concerned." he said later, "with saving the wilderness than in getting a law passed saying that I had done so." Or to quote S. Herbert Evison, who served for many years in the National Park Service: "We who have tried to improve conditions have been too ready to compromise. Experience shows it is better to make demands than deals."

In Brandborg's case, the test came in consideration before Congress of the official proposal for designation of the San Rafael Wilderness in California, the first national forest area to be reviewed after passage of the 1964 act. The Forest Service proposed a wilderness of 143,000 acres, but the California Citizens Committee for the San Rafael Wilderness felt it must hold its ground for an additional 2,200 acres. The contested area covered an unusual meadow life zone, highlighted by *potreros*, or grassy balds, dotted with rocky outcrops, a beautiful, unworldly scene. Inscribed among the rocks were prehistoric aboriginal cave art, considered among the best yet discovered in North America. After a hard fight in Congress, the Forest Service had its way, but it was worth the fight, for Brandborg showed the local activists that he and the Wilderness Society would stick with them on principle.

I recall also Brandborg's role at the first public hearing on wilderness in the national parks, dealing with Great Smoky Mountains National Park and conducted at Gatlinburg, Tennessee, in 1966. The agency offered a dreadful plan, of road construction and massive campgrounds designed to intrude upon instead of protecting wilderness. Harvey Broome, president of the Wilderness Society, and his friend and hiking partner, Ernest Dickerman, both of whom lived in nearby Knoxville, mobilized the local citizens and coordinated with Brandborg to make a national issue of the Smoky Mountains wilderness.

Brandborg set the tone for the hearing at Gatlinburg when he said:

"Conservationists the world over are looking to our National Park Service for exemplary leadership in safeguarding the beauty and character of natural landscape. It would be most unfortunate if the Park Service were unable to fulfill this role in the Smokies." Others followed. "No road on earth is important enough to destroy the values inherent in these mountains," warned one of many scientists who testified. "Saving the wilderness may be one of the few worthwhile accomplishments of this generation," said a young mother. Witness after witness identified with love of land, idealism, the qualitative experience that must be the essence of our national parks.

The fight to protect the Smokies from their protectors continued until 1971, when the Park Service issued a new report, withdrawing its proposal for a new transmountain highway and conceding that the Smokies comprise "a natural treasure of plant and animal life living in an ecological balance that once destroyed can never be restored."

Dickerman was impressive and effective during the Smokies fight and Brandborg hired him to conduct local leadership training programs for the Wilderness Society. He was typical of personnel on the staff. They didn't work for the money, they worked for the cause. Or, as Dickerman wrote to me years later:

It is the volunteers back home, the grassroots, who fundamentally get the job done. Sure, we need the national organizations and their staffs to carry the message to Congress and the agencies, no question; the direct human contact is essential. I am glad that you and I were most active directly in an earlier time when for the most part the spirit was pure and the cause felt personally!

And when Brandborg left the Wilderness Society, Dickerman left too. For Brandborg, the parting in January 1976 was unhappy and acrimonious, for he actually was discharged by the governing council that he had long served. His dismissal was explained later as a very small part of a very long article on the history of the Wilderness Society published in *Wilderness* (formerly *Living Wilderness*) for winter 1984. The author brushed off Brandborg's role in the fight for wilderness, asserting that his work was marked by "operating at too fevered an emotional pitch," and that he gave too much attention to Alaska and not enough to the western field staff of the Society."

Dave Foreman, who had begun his environmental career on that western field staff, was appalled and furious. In January 1986 he dashed off a hot letter to the author, Stephen Fox. Yes, conceded Foreman, there was dissatisfaction among the staff because of Brandborg's commitment to Alaska, but that commitment clearly made the oil pipeline to the North Slope much safer and led to "the tremendous effort to safeguard over 100 million acres of parks, refuges and wild rivers in Alaska." Foreman summarized his feeling: "Stewart Brandborg is a great man in American conservation, full of vision, courage and a solid environmental ethic."

That is the way I see him too, though I know Brandborg in a very personal way through long years of friendship and plead guilty to bias. Like all the rest of us, he has his weaknesses. Verbal overkill is one of them – that is, where one word will do he is likely to use two, or three. Sigurd Olson, the author, was a friend and strong supporter, but once struck back at the long and wordy letters he received: "Brandy, if you can't say it in one page, don't say it!"

But for commitment and courage in the crunch and unflagging energy to mobilize the troops, Brandborg stands at the head of the class. Leaving the Wilderness Society was not the end but a new beginning. He went to work organizing Conservationists for Carter, a national network that may well have made the difference in Jimmy Carter's victory over Gerald Ford. Then he served in the government as special assistant to the director of the National Park Service, showing parks people how to relate to citizen activists.

Ultimately, after Ronald Reagan was elected president and James G. Watt took over the Department of the Interior, Brandborg returned home – home to the Bitterroot Valley of western Montana, where he grew up and attended school, and where he met and courted his wife of fifty years. He and Anna Vee live with two dogs and a parrot in a handsome log home on a hill with vistas of mountain wilderness in all directions, where their five grown children and families are in and out and friends come to call from all over. The house where they live is definitely a happy home.

Part of the happiness derives from Brandborg's continued activism and involvement. The phone is always busy with affairs of the Friends of the Bitterroot, Wilderness Watch and even, these days, the Wilderness Society. Stewart Brandborg may be in his mid-70s, but he is still going strong, looking toward the future rather than living in the past. I must say, however, that he has accounted for some choice hours in conservation history and given me personal memories to cherish.

Wilderness Watch, 1999.

17. "In wildness is the preservation of the world "

"In wildness is the preservation of the world." With those eight simple words Henry David Thoreau defined for his time and all time a specific and inescapable social responsibility. Thoreau, however, had no way of foreseeing the state of the world as we know it now in the last decade of the Twentieth Century: a planet deeply wounded, troubled by pollution, overpopulation, corruption, violence, and widening disparity between the riches of the rich and impoverishment of the poor, the manifest ills of a technological supercivilization dangerously out of control.

For our particular period, I would add to Thoreau that in the preservation of wild nature lies individual salvation. I don't mean in wildness alone, but in the conscious effort to preserve and perpetuate wildness, for nature and humankind, after all, are indivisible.

"Only in acts of articulate compassion, in rare and hidden moments of communion with nature," wrote Loren Eisely, "does man briefly escape his solitary destiny." Yes, those rare, hidden moments in communion with nature are essential to rediscover the soul and rekindle the spirit, but no less so is the expression of articulate compassion that we celebrate in Earth Day 1990.

In this spirit I review the past and look to the future, with wilderness protected under provisions of the Wilderness Act as a symbol of hope and reason, of respect for the earth as the source of respect for each other. I see the Wilderness Act as a beginning, or a step along the way, rather than an end in itself. Since 1964, more than 100 items of wilderness legislation have been passed by Congress, including the Eastern Wilderness Act of 1975, designating key tracts in the East, the Federal Land Policy and Management Act of 1976, extending the wilderness system to include areas administered by the Bureau of Land Management, and the Alaska National Interest Lands Conservation Act of 1980, adding more than 60 million acres to the system.

Those are positive achievements, enabling us to feel uplifted today by inspiration from the principled, selfless, and far-seeing leaders in the wilderness crusade of a generation ago. They were caring, sharing and giving, articulate and compassionate. I feel privileged to have known many of them, and privileged anew to relate their work and vision to an upcoming generation of leaders and activists.

Nevertheless, Earth Day 1990 should be the time to identify the unfinished agenda, recognizing chronic weak spots and new opportunities. I remember the words of Senator Clinton P. Anderson at the dedication in 1954 of the Aldo Leopold Memorial at the portal to the Gila National Wilderness in New Mexico. The Gila thirty years before had become the first designated wilderness, resulting entirely from Leopold's initiative as a Forest Service official in the Southwest. Senator Anderson spoke of the creative commitment of his old friend (who had died in 1948) and then declared:

> We now become trustees of his inheritance. Those of us who may visit within the wilderness have an obligation to see that the work of one generation shall not be sacrificed by those who come after. We have an obligation to make sure that this area may remain untouched, for generations and perhaps centuries to come.

Though I was not present at the scene, Senator Anderson later told me of his conversations with Leopold about wilderness, enlisting him in the cause of preservation. I treasure such connections with wilderness advocates, and feel fortunate to have been an observer and recorder of momentous events, and in a small way a participant in them. My personal experience and readings convince me that preservation of wild places is the best of American traditions. Wilderness is at the heart of the nation. It tells one generation what is right and lasting about all generations and about the land itself.

"Now we face the question of whether a still 'higher standard of living' is worth its cost in things natural, wild and free," wrote Leopold, but he was by no means first with this idea. William Penn, even in the colonial period, wanted one acre of forest left wild for every five acres that were cleared. Thoreau had the same idea. "A town is saved," he wrote in the nineteenth century, "not more by the righteous men in it than by the woods that surround it."

New York State moved to save the best of its wild heritage in 1892 by establishing the Adirondack Park, then following up two years later with a constitutional amendment declaring that: "The lands of the state, now owned or hereafter acquired, constituting the forest preserve as now fixed by law, shall be kept forever as wild forest lands. They shall not be leased, sold, or exchanged, or be taken by any corporation, public or private, nor shall the timber thereon be sold, removed, or destroyed."

Those citations are well recorded, but I continually discover new evidence of public care and concern. During the four years I spent in Idaho, for example, I came across documents showing that in the late 1920s the governor of the state appointed a committee to consider the wisdom of establishing something to be called a "primitive area" in the national forests of central Idaho. After three years of consultation and study, the regional forester proposed to close approximately one million acres to public roads, buildings and other permanent improvements. The idea received support from all quarters. The chairman of the governor's committee, representing the timber industry, was its strongest booster.

Consequently, early in 1931 chief forester Robert Y. Stuart approved establishment of the Idaho Primitive Area (in due course to become the Frank Church-River of No Return Wilderness), stating: "The potential value of the Idaho Primitive Area for recreational and inspirational purposes is greater, more susceptible of early realization and more desirable than is the utilization of its material resources."

There was no input, so far as I can determine, from Aldo Leopold, or from the other two Forest Service wilderness pioneers, Arthur Carhart and Robert Marshall. It was essentially a local show, the outcome of a movement on the part of people who care, in collaboration with the resource professionals, who were largely a different breed in those days.

I knew Carhart in his later years, before his death in 1978, and wish he was more widely appreciated. In 1919, as the first landscape architect hired by the Forest Service, he convinced his superiors that the Trappers Lake area of the White River National Forest in Colorado should remain roadless rather than be made accessible for summer homes. That, as far as I can tell, was the first definitive application of the wilderness idea. Later he did much the same for the Superior National Forest in Minnesota, identifying a large area that could be "as priceless as Yellowstone, Yosemite, or the Grand Canyon – if it remained a water-trail wilderness." It was the beginning of the Boundary Waters Canoe Area Wilderness, renowned because it remains roadless.

Marshall, as chief of recreation in the Forest Service, enlarged national forest wilderness and strengthened regulations to protect it, although his interests cut across bureaucratic boundaries of federal lands. He related actively to progressive citizen concern and was the prime mover in organizing the Wilderness Society. His brother George shared with me a copy of *The People's Forests*, a wonderful little book written by Robert Marshall in 1933, well deserving of reissue today. In it he proposed a national network of numerous reservations located in all sections of the country, both to make them accessible and to avoid overuse. He defined wilderness in words that ultimately would be strongly reflected in the Wilderness Act (though it came into law 25 years after his death in 1939).

But everywhere in the country wilderness came under attack, pressured by road-building, dam-building, logging, mining, recreation and tourism, those goodies of modern times. Even the Gila Wilderness was threatened by the proposed Hooker Dam. Nor were the national parks any longer safe – it actually took a nationwide campaign to convince Congress to keep dams out of the Grand Canyon.

"How Much Wilderness Can We Afford to Lose?" Such was the challenge raised by Howard Zahniser in 1951 at the Second Biennial Wilderness Conference of the Sierra Club. Zahniser saw test cases everywhere – so widespread that citizen conservationists were continually on the defensive. He called for a bold strategy, an offensive to establish a national wilderness preservation system composed of lands administered by federal agencies.

Zahniser as executive director of the Wilderness Society led the offensive. "We are not fighting progress," he would say. "We are making it. We are not dealing with a vanishing wilderness. We are working for a wilderness forever."

In those days the Wilderness Society was a small organization with a small staff operating in humble quarters, but emboldened by a sense of a grand mission. I think of such highly committed people as Michael Nadel, who at one period in his life had initiated and conducted conservation programs for urban children and who had worked for years on wilderness preservation in the Adirondacks, and Stewart Brandborg, who grew up with the great Idaho-Montana wilderness as his backyard. Once I asked Brandy if he had met Robert Marshall. "But, of course," he answered. "There was the time Bob made his solo hike over the mountains and came to our house, when my father worked on the Nez Perce National Forest."

Brandy logged considerable solo time in the mountains, too, particularly during his field study of mountain goats while a graduate wildlife student at the University of Idaho. He was Zahnie's protege and successor when Zahnie died a few months before passage of the Wilderness Act.

Then there were the field crusaders – individuals like Olaus Murie, who knew the wilderness intimately from his scientific expeditions, a wonderful wildlife artist though he never studied art, and his wife, Margaret, or "Mardy," one of the great women of our time, who still inspires anyone fortunate enough to meet her or to read her written works; and Sigurd Olson, wilderness guide and educator, who at the age of 50 began his creative writing career, enduring many, many rejection slips en route to producing his classics about the north woods canoe wilderness; and Harvey Broome, my own special mentor, who set aside his law career for his love of wilderness, and without whose concern and leadership the Great Smoky Mountains National Park would now be laced with highways. Harvey taught me many lessons, including the need to resist any and all development within wilderness, for slow attrition inevitably follows. "It must be clear," said Harvey, "that the demand which now looms over us can never be satisfied. To protect what is left we must live with the facilities we now have. The hardest thing will be the decision itself."

Another was William O. Douglas, whose entire life stands as a record of courage, a willingness to go it alone against heavy odds. As a sickly child he gained health and inspiration by hiking in the wild Cascades of Washington State. Years later he brought a wilderness conscience to Washington, D.C. with his celebrated hike along the Chesapeake & Ohio Canal.

Through association with such people of bright mind and elevated spirit, I learned that when one person sets his or her sights higher and articulates true compassion, others can hardly fail to be moved. In this respect, I will cite the case of Representative John P. Saylor, of Pennsylvania, the author of the Wilderness Bill on the House side. The first bill was introduced in 1956 by one Democratic senator, Hubert Humphrey, of Minnesota, with eight co-sponsors, and one Republican House member, Saylor. Between June 1957 and May 1964, eighteen hearings were held on the wilderness proposal in both Washington and the West. The bill was passed by the Senate April 10,1963, by a vote of 73-12, with Clinton Anderson, of New Mexico, and Frank Church, of Idaho, the floor leader, playing key roles. It was a different story on the House side, where the bill was bottled up year after year by Wayne Aspinall, of Colorado, the powerful, crusty chairman of the Interior Committee.

The extractive industries that felt public lands were their private domain fought it tooth-and-toenail. The Forest Service and National Park Service fought it, too, in the true spirit of bureaucracy entrenched. Saylor, however, a towering figure of indomitable will, never gave up. Finally Aspinall acceded: the bill was passed by the House July 30,1964, with only one negative vote and was signed by President Lyndon B. Johnson in the White House rose garden on September 3, 1964.

Passage of the Wilderness Act opened an age of environmental awareness and activism, inspiring many people to continue the crusade. I went to California to hike in the San Rafael Wilderness, the first area reviewed under the 1964 act. My companion was Dick Smith, an energetic Santa Barbara newsman who made the Los Padres National Forest his special beat. He knew the area intimately and championed its protection. When he died suddenly in 1977, the mayor proclaimed Dick Smith Week and the whole community mourned. Dick had helped to get a large roadless area adjacent to the San Rafael placed on the wilderness study list – a mosaic of chaparral slopes, Indian cave paintings, sandstone cliffs, and 6,541-foot Madulce Peak – and in 1981 it was named the Dick Smith Wilderness. Rather like Carhart in northern Minnesota and Aldo Leopold in the brushy Southwest, Smith saw something special others had missed.

The historic act of 1964 established a definition of wilderness in law and a National Wilderness Preservation System in fact. It was imperfect on passage, allowing mineral exploration through December 31, 1983, and it remains imperfect today. But the wilderness system has grown and endured, outlasting Reagan-Watt attempts to undermine it, and the principle of wilderness preservation is firmly established the world over.

The passage of the Wilderness Act, despite the opposition of commercial interests and entrenched bureaucracy, demonstrates that Americans are not crass, dollar-minded or exploitation-conscious. They were not in 1964 and are not today, as evidenced by the continued expansion of the National Wilderness Preservation System. Too often Americans have allowed powerful self-serving interests to control decision-making, but when presented with strong valid ideas in the common good they respond with approval and support. A review of wilderness history thus teaches that each of us must be inspired to realize the power of his or her own life and to never sell it short. The timid, the hesitant, the compromisers have failed. The bigger and bolder the program, the greater the chance of success. Individually and collectively, true believers can and do work miracles, if we have faith and hang together, daring to take risks based on principle above political expediency.

The work of the wilderness crusaders of yesteryear inspires succeeding generations to safeguard the national treasures identified and defined in the Wilderness Act. For all of our public lands, wilderness in particular, comprise the most priceless possessions we Americans share as a people.

No other country is so enriched by its parks, forests, wildlife refuges and other reserves administered by towns, cities, counties, states and the federal government. Land is wealth, and we the people ought to hold onto every acre of it in the common interest. Public lands provide roving room, a sense of freedom and release from urbanized high-tech supercivilization. Without public lands there would be no place of substance left for wildlife, which has shared our heritage since time immemorial.

Yet no administration in my lifetime, and quite possibly none in the long history of the Republic, manifested greater antagonism and hostility to the principle of public land than the recent administration of Ronald Reagan. He came to Washington as a self-proclaimed Sagebrush Rebel, surrounding himself with a band of anti-federal zealots like James G. Watt, determined to dismember and "privatize" the federal estate. They left behind a dismal legacy.

George Bush led us to believe that his administration would be different. I felt cheered when he introduced the environmental issue into the 1988 presidential campaign, pledging himself to be an environmental president in the tradition of Theodore Roosevelt. Those words were easy, however. We can see a few improvements, but mostly on the surface. Bush & Company may speak of excellence, but the administration has given us a shallow, ill-informed Secretary of the Interior, plus a rerun of the Reagan wrecking crew, with many of the old crowd still on board.

The Forest Service is in bad enough shape already. It has lost its way as a professional agency. I speak with many retirees and personnel in the ranks. They are deeply distressed with the lack of courageous leadership and direction from their own leaders. Little remains of the spark and purpose once evoked by Gifford Pinchot with bold ideas and expressions, such as: "The earth belongs by right to all its people and not to a minority, insignificant in number but tremendous in wealth and power." The Forest Service under Pinchot achieved its reputation for square-shooting and fearlessness in a system then – as now – constipated with bureaucracy, bungling and timidity. "It is the honorable distinction of the Forest Service," Pinchot wrote, "that it has been more constantly, more violently and more bitterly attacked by the representatives of the special interests than any other government bureau. These attacks have increased in violence and bitterness in proportion as the Service has offered opposition to predatory wealth."

I wish that "honorable distinction" was being earned anew, yesterday or today, but no such luck. The Forest Service is out of touch with the environmental age, out of touch with the idea expressed by Senator Hubert Humphrey in connection with the National Forest Management Act of 1976. "The days have ended when the forest may be viewed only as trees and trees viewed only as timber," Humphrey said. "The soil and water, the grasses and shrubs, the fish and the wildlife, and the beauty that is the forest must become integral parts of resource managers' thinking and action."

The Forest Service is out of touch because, I fear, Chief Dale Robertson himself is out of touch. He believes that all goes well with business as usual in the same old way. He likes to call the Forest Service "the number one supplier of outdoor recreation in the United States," as though numbers count most, when the truth is that his outfit has been doing a poor job in recreation. Recreation for years has come in last, in funding, and in status up and down the line. The chief talks about a new priority in recreation, which may sound promising on the face of it, but, in fact, decision-makers in his agency time after time follow a course of roading and logging that utterly eliminates choice recreation sites from the national forests.

Chief Robertson now speaks about furnishing "all-American recreation experiences," specifically with more roads for motoring and more ski slopes for downhill skiing, with scant concern for the impact of these activities on the resources. The chief is playing a dangerous game, endeavoring to find public support by appealing to the lowest common denominator of public taste, inviting a gross misuse of public lands.

Chief Robertson and the Forest Service leadership around him show little personal feeling or love for the land. They show scant appreciation of plants, animals, soils, geology, or human history associated with the areas in their charge.

Little wonder that on March 15, 1989, Representative Bruce Vento, Chairman of the House Subcommittee on National Parks and Public

Lands, addressed a stern letter to Chief Robertson, following an extensive review by his Committee of National Forest Wilderness Management. Representative Vento cited these findings:

> Many national forest wilderness areas are being damaged. Trails and campsites are suffering from inadequate planning, construction, mainte-nance, reconstruction, and rehabilitation. Meadows are being overgrazed by ranchers and by outfitters. Inappropriate 'privatization' through camp-site reservations and quasi-permanent facilities is being allowed. The public and even agency personnel are conducting activities inside wilder-ness boundaries that are in violation of the Wilderness Act.

The record of the National Park Service is no better. Its leaders resis-ted the Wilderness Act, contending it was already protecting wilderness under its organic legislation. History has shown this is not the case: In the early 1970s the agency leadership proposed wilderness "enclaves" and "corridors" in the hope of allowing intrusive lodgings and tramways. In more recent years political influences have transformed a professional bureau into a political bureau emphasizing recreational tourism, complete with urban malls, supermarkets, airplanes and helicopters sightseeing overhead, snowmobiling and other motorized activity and artificiality in wild country.

Wilderness has been given low priority. Many National Park Service officials have lost the ability to cope with nature preservation on a large scale – they fail to recognize that roads and hotels and "pleasuring" can be as destructive to wilderness in national parks as clearcut logging is in national forests. It approaches the scandalous that in 1990, more than twenty-five years after passage of the Wilderness Act, national parks like Yellowstone and Grand Canyon still do not contain an acre of classified wilderness.

The central issue as I see it is not management, but the values sought through public policy and defined by it. Land use embodies both science and philosophy, but the philosophy is more important by far. It must come first, based on love of the earth and respect for all creatures with which we share it. How to utilize wilderness, and public lands in general, as an edu-cational and inspirational resource so that oncoming generations respect the natural world is part of the fundamental challenge as we look ahead to the next twenty-five years and beyond.

We need to learn much more about wilderness: where it is and where it was; its physical and psychic therapeutic qualities; its relation to science, art, ethics, and religion; the contributions of individuals who have helped, in their own way, to save it and give meaning to it for society. Since I have been invited to talk of history, let me introduce the name of Samuel H. Boardman, known as "father of the Oregon state parks system," and recount an intriguing episode of Western conservation history.

After his retirement in 1950 at the age of seventy-six, Sam Boardman spent a part of each day, until he died in 1953, writing historic and descriptive sketches of those wonderful state parks. One of the sketches, titled "How a state park was acquired by Washington and missed by Oregon," dealt with Beacon Rock, located 40 miles up the Columbia River Gorge from Vancouver, Washington. Beacon Rock, an imposing geologic feature, stands 900 feet high and is considered second only to Gibraltar in monolithic stature. In 1931, an entrepreneur proposed to take it apart as a source of rock for a jetty being built at the mouth of the Columbia. Sam was concerned: The scenic preservation of the rock meant as much to Oregon as to Washington. It had been offered to Washington as a gift, but Washington didn't want it.

Sam contacted the owner and determined that it might indeed be given to Oregon. He immediately reported to the chairman of the highway commission, a man who was very enthusiastic about parks; in fact, his commission had organized the parks department. "I greeted the chairman with the information that we had a new park," wrote Sam. "His face wreathed in smiles. 'What is it, Sam?' 'Beacon Rock.' The smiles went into a grimace; from his lips there sizzled, 'You are crazy as hell.'"

But Sam persisted. The legislature could pass a law whereby the state was free to accept the gift. "Why should we let the width of a river," reasoned Sam, "destroy a scenic asset woven into a recreational garland belonging to both states? How could we stand by and see the death of a relative, though a bit distant? If such things of beauty were not fought to a saving conclusion, then the waters of Multnomah Falls would be falling through steel pipes for the generation of electricity."

The chairman relented to the extent of giving news of the gift to the Portland papers. The *Oregonian* editorialized: "So far as we know, no state in the union now owns a park in another state. It is a gift unprecedented and as such, whether Oregon accepts it or not, is likely to arouse a stronger public interest in this natural monument. It would be a sad commentary upon the intelligence of the people of this section if it be permitted to fall into selfish hands."

That did it. Home pride in the state of Washington was rekindled through the effrontery of a bordering state. "The Rock is saved to posterity," Sam exulted in his memoir. "It is now developed and used by many. While not under the jurisdiction of Oregon, it is ours to see and wonder at its birth."

That lovely expression and Sam's bold initiative reflect an ethic, a desire, a passion, a degree of professionalism that rises above profession, an enthusiasm for life and for human purpose. Sam Boardman's strong feeling derived from homeland love, homeland pride, an affinity for wild nature, a yearning to protect and preserve as part of contemporary civilization.

Wild nature is that way. Wild nature is the source of inspiration in art and literature, of feeling for oneself, for others, for all of life. Those who study the human condition have given strong supporting testimony. "It is a commonplace of all religious thought, even the most primitive," wrote Loren Eisely, "that the man seeking vision and insight must go apart from his fellows and live for a time in the wilderness." Loren described the loneliness of humankind in the universe, then adding: "Only in acts of articulate compassion, in rare and hidden moments of communion with nature, does man briefly escape his solitary destiny."

Thomas Merton told it a little differently: of his discovery of new perceptions once he was free of social standards and values he found repugnant, of a society happy because it drinks Coca-Cola or Seagram's, or both, and is protected by the bomb, a society imaged in the mass media, advertising, movies, TV, best sellers, and current fads, all the pompous and trifling masks with which it hides its callousness, sensuality, hypocrisy, cruelty, and fear. No art form stirred him more deeply than paleolithic cave painting, with its dynamic power, vitality, and self-realization, an expression of direct awareness, a celebration of the wholeness of communion with nature and with life.

Joseph Wood Krutch also discovered new perceptions once he was liberated from old constraints. As a New York high brow, he was cranky, sick, and unfulfilled, but after moving to the Southwest in 1952, his outlook changed. His biographer, John D. Margolis, describes the transformation:

> His life had ceased to strive for effects. He had ceased straining, and
> at last was living authentically. No elaborate psychosomatic theory is
> required to see a connection between emotional distress and physical

illness. The uneasiness Krutch felt with his New York career had its counterpart in a chronic malaise. It was hardly coincidental – and a result of something more than the Arizona climate – that Krutch enjoyed more consistent good health than he had since his youth. The desert became a temple, where the former agnostic, now a pantheist, went to worship.

In his New York days Krutch wore the pose of an intellectual elitist. In Arizona he undoubtedly learned a great deal while writing his biography of Thoreau; he wanted to show that each and every person could enjoy experiences like his. "By contact with the living nature," wrote Krutch, "we are reminded of the mysterious, nonmechanical aspects of the living organism. By such contact we begin to get, even in contemplating nature's lowest forms, a sense of the mystery, the independence, the unpredictableness of the living as opposed to the mechanical. And it is upon the recognition of these characteristics that he shares with all living creatures that any recognition of man's dignity has to be based."

The public, unfortunately, has been led to believe by Congress, the federal agencies and major conservation organizations that once an area is designated as wilderness everything will be fine. But things don't work that way. Many wilderness areas are abused and degraded, often by uncontrolled and inappropriate recreation uses; they are staffed by inadequate personnel insufficiently trained.

The agencies simply do not take their responsibility seriously. The decision makers, mostly trained in vocational forestry schools, view the earth as a composite of commodities intended for consumption; they have little appreciation of wilderness, if any at all. The Forest Service is oriented to timber, the Bureau of Land Management to grazing and mining, the Fish and Wildlife Service to ducks and deer for hunters, and the National Park Service to crowds and tourism.

Yes, there are able, wilderness-conscious, ecosystem-conscious people at work in these agencies, but they often do their best against heavy odds. They are frustrated and unfulfilled. The agencies provide policy statements, manuals, plans and promises proclaiming the future of wilderness, but the documentation is mostly bureaucratic paperwork. Good people in the ranks want to do more; they deserve a better break.

I propose a place for them – through a very separate branch of government outside the land management structure, a new agency, to be called the United States Wilderness Service. Since we pay people in government to serve mining, oil and gas, electric power, grazing, logging, and other resource-consumptive interests, why not underwrite a cadre of men and women who will prove the government responsive to the people's wilderness cause?

The Wilderness Service would undertake many missions now unmet. For example, the Wilderness Act directs administrators to gather and disseminate information on the use of wilderness, but this is not done, or done poorly at best. This would be one of the main activities of the Wilderness Service. Conceiving wilderness in its broadest sense, it would explore and illuminate uses relative to wildlife, plantlife, archaeology, history, art, literature, and philosophy, treating them as cultural resources rather than as commodities.

The Wilderness Service would be deeply involved in research into the values of specific ecological types, the threats they face, and the steps required to save them. No bureau performs that kind of service today.

The Wilderness Act furnishes the process for preservation of large tracts of federal lands. But the Wilderness Service would be responsible for a coordinated approach beyond this scope. Some states, inspired by the act, have developed their own initiatives in preservation. They need an exchange of data and other states deserve the chance to benefit from their accumulated experience. For that matter, other nations in the world, having followed our lead in national parks and wildlife conservation, should be able to learn how wilderness is saved and administered, with technical aid to help them.

Federal land management agencies cannot perform these functions. Their approaches are too narrow and the efforts of their wilderness-oriented personnel are circumscribed. But the new agency, vitalized with the energy and imagination of these people in its fold, and with the single, specific mandate of wilderness, would be the ideal vehicle.

The Wilderness Service, as I perceive it, would not administer land, but it would furnish new ideas for better land administration. It would help to set standards for the amount and types of human use an area can absorb without impairing its wild quality, hopefully reversing the widespread trend of deterioration and degradation.

We can never allocate enough wilderness, but we should continually improve the administration of areas in the wilderness system. Earth Day 1990 marks a fitting point to re-consider the propriety and proportions of such activities as grazing, hunting, fishing and trapping; fire control; insect and disease control; luxury outfitting with permanent and semi-permanent structures, and aircraft flights over wilderness.

Let us advance the ethical cause by redefining the purpose of all public lands, of reassessing what they do to enrich life in America, in long-range terms of economics, science, and recreation, and beyond them of culture, art and spirituality. Emerson wrote that literature, poetry and science are all homage of humans to the unfathomed secrets of nature.

Places of scenic beauty do not increase, but on the contrary are being reduced in number and diminished in quality. Our responsibility is to see that future generations enjoy the same opportunity accessible to us for solitude and the same sense that nature, rather than humankind, prevails.

The time is long overdue to apply the principle of stewardship, real stewardship, to our entire planet, with public lands in the United States as the exemplars. Society should have its choices, but one choice should be wilderness, whether embodied in a single plant or a great virgin forest, whether a desert or a mountain, a California condor, grizzly bear, or spotted owl, but that image is possible because somewhere that image exists in fact. There can never be enough of it.

I see wilderness as sanctuary of the spirit, the heart of a moral world governed by peace and love. Nuclear weapons will never force nations to join in recognizing the limitations of a fragile earth. Stealth bombers and Trident submarines cannot bring people together as brothers and sisters caring for each other in our common destiny. We should give up the illusion of military solutions and redirect funding, personnel and energy to constructive humanitarian purposes. Let us commemorate Earth Day 1990 with yet a new beginning on a broad front, and pledge allegiance to a green and peaceful planet. For in wildness is the preservation of the world.

In Celebration of Earth Day 1990, at a symposium at Utah State University.

18. Afoul of lumber barons and politicians: Charles H. Stoddard

Over the years I met and worked with good, able people like Chuck Stoddard. Now, along with all the previously published materials in this collection, I elected to include this letter to Chuck's son, Glenn, an attorney in Madison, Wisconsin.

August 19, 1998
Mr. Glenn M. Stoddard
Madison, Wisconsin

Dear Glenn:

On reading the article about your father's passing in the *Boundary Waters Wilderness News*, I thought I should write a few words for the Stoddard clan about Chuck as I knew him.

I respected and admired Chuck. He was endowed with strong progressive principles of public service that made him selfless and fearless. He never received the credit in the public arena that he deserved.

But then, he wasn't looking for credit. In the book *Westward in Eden*, William K. Wyant wrote of how "Stoddard, outspoken by BLM standards, ran afoul of lumber barons and politicians during a controversy over a land swap involving BLM acreage in Oregon." Wyant called him "dynamic and brilliant, but impatient." I believe that he was impatient only with laxity and wrongdoing. As Chuck himself wrote in a report following his departure from BLM, "A showing of strength meant controversy and in the Department of the Interior controversy has always been shunned whenever powerful interest groups brought on political pressure." In short, he put his own career on the block for a cause that was clearly right.

Chuck was highly regarded and was always there when needed. The article in the newsletter failed to mention his constructive role as chairman of the governing council of the Wilderness Society during a difficult period in that organization's history or his role as chairman of an advisory committee trying to build environmental responsibility into programs and policies of the US Army Corps of Engineers. In the book *Sterile Forest: The Case Against Clearcutting*, Edward C. Fritz wrote of Chuck's testimony in a trial in Texas endeavoring to prevent wholesale overcutting of national forests in that state. The author concluded the relevant section of the book as follows:

> As Stoddard stepped down from the witness stand, I accompanied him to the door and thanked him for a task well done. Stoddard rushed away to Dallas to catch the earliest possible plane for Duluth and his home country. He had given to the cause exactly what was needed.

I was privileged two or three times to visit Chuck at the home place at Minong, Wisconsin, where he practiced forestry and proved that it works on the selective system without cutting down the whole forest. He was a great forester and a great guy. I valued him as a friend. I think your brother Jeffrey was wrong when he wrote there was no place in Chuck's style for "etiquette, small talk and pleasantries." I found him always to be courteous, gracious, respectful of people, and I enjoyed small talk, pleasantries and good humor in his company, whether at the Cosmos Club, which he made his headquarters in Washington, or at Minong, or wherever. But of course Jeffrey was absolutely right in citing your father's "lifelong dedication to do what was right and what was honorable." That is how we most remember Chuck Stoddard.

With best,
Michael Frome

* * * * * *

A few more words are in order here.

Charles H. Stoddard was trained as a forester and social scientist. He was the author of *Essentials of Forestry Practice*, the fourth edition of which is still in print, and *Looking Forward* (MacMillan, 1982), a LaFollette-like progressive view of economic and social issues. Following the election of President John F. Kennedy in 1962, Stoddard served on the executive staff of Interior Secretary Stewart L. Udall. When Udall appointed him director of the Bureau of Land Management, he vowed to break the power and influence of corporate grazing and logging over the public lands.

Ultimately "he ran afoul of lumber barons and politicians" in Oregon and was forced to resign, after which he returned to the upper Midwest, his home country, as a citizen activist. In 1976, he was called by Edward C. Fritz, mentioned above, to testify in a law suit against the Forest Service in Texas. Fritz himself was a lawyer of means who had quit his practice to crusade for conservation. Through the Texas Committee on Natural Resources, he sued the Forest Service, charging the agency was actually damaging the forests in its charge by overcutting and clearcutting. He introduced various professional specialists including Stoddard in forestry and others in recreation, ornithology, botany, ecology and economics.

On March 24, 1977, Judge William Wayne Justice ruled for the plaintiff, finding the Forest Service had violated laws and trust, and had seriously impaired recreation, wildlife and soil conservation. He enjoined the Forest Service from any further clearcut logging on Texas national forests. The government appealed and won on grounds the court had improperly substituted its judgment for that of the technical experts of the agency. That did not make much sense to me at the time, and still doesn't today, beyond proving anew how tough it is to fight city hall. Fritz documented the whole case in his book *Sterile Forest*, published by Eakin Press, Austin, in 1983.

19. *Heal the earth,*
Heal the soul

On the day in 1968 that Martin Luther King, Jr. was shot and killed in Memphis, I was at Yale University to speak on conservation policy, certainly including the preservation of wilderness. Once alone following the program, I felt deeply disturbed, trying to equate my actions and personal goals with the tragedy and meaning of Dr. King's life. I asked myself then (and many times since) whether environmentalism and wilderness can be valid in the face of poverty, inequality, and other critical social issues.

The ghetto is a symbol of modern environmental disaster. On one hand, the affluent escape crowds, concrete, and crime by moving to the suburbs. They breathe cleaner air in a cleaner environment. On the other hand, the poor, especially the nonwhite, cannot make it. They are disenfranchised from the bounties of our time. The lower the income, the lower the quality of life, but the higher the air pollution and the diseases from it.

I learned an important lesson in Memphis. I had been there before Dr. King's death and had written about the conservation efforts of a hardy group called the Citizens to Preserve Overton Park. On the face of it, the Citizens had nothing in common with the humble black garbage workers whose cause Dr. King had come to defend. Or perhaps they did, considering they were fighting exactly the same economic and political forces.

Overton at that time had already been a park for almost seventy years. Though less than half the size of Central Park in New York, the woodlands of Overton Park, with seventy-five varieties of trees, are probably richer. It is, in fact, one of the few urban forests left in the world. However, when downtown merchants and developers decided that a freeway through the park would jingle coins in their pockets, the distinctive urban forest became expendable. The two Memphis daily newspapers led the battle for the freeway, belittling any politician who dared stand up in behalf of the park. A former mayor of the city, Watkins Overton, great-grandson of the man for whom the park was named, courageously spoke of the park as hallowed ground – a priceless possession of the people beyond commercial value. Nevertheless, he and the upper side of Memphis learned painfully, along with the garbage workers, that democracy can be "a government of bullies." As Overton said, "Entrenched bureaucracy disdains the voice of the people but eventually the people will be heard."

That idea is paramount in my mind. Entrenched bureaucracy of all kinds disdains the voice of the people. It is the weakness of institutions, whether private or public, profit-making or eleemosynary, academic or professional. Institutions, by their nature, tend to breed conformity and compliance; the older and larger it becomes, the less vision the institution expresses or tolerates. But eventually the people will be heard, as evidenced in the ultimately successful efforts of both the garbage workers and the defenders of Overton Park.

The pioneer ecologist Paul Sears said, "Conservation is a point of view involved with the concept of freedom, human dignity, and the American spirit." Gifford Pinchot expressed the same idea. "The rightful use and purpose of our natural resources," he said, is "to make all the people strong and well, able and wise, well-taught, well-fed ... full of knowledge and initiative, with equal opportunity for all and special privilege for none." He conceived forestry as the vanguard of a public crusade against control of government by big business. Under his leadership the Forest Service achieved an early reputation for fearlessness in a system then, as now, constipated with bureaucracy, bungling, and timidity. How times have changed! Pinchot stressed the cause of forestry education to train professionals in a social movement; but foresters today are technical people, focused mostly on wood production, trained to see trees as board feet of timber, which is how the Forest Service conducts its business in the public forests.

The National Park Service is not much different. Its personnel may voice concern for ecology as a principle, but scarcely as something practical in critical need of defense. The best defense, at least in my view, is an alert and alarmed public. But national parks personnel are generally inward-oriented and poor communicators. They know the public as visitor numbers, but not as decision makers. Woe unto the parks person who goes to the public with faith or trust in his or her heart. The parks person is a "professional," which is how he or she learned to appreciate the values of ecology in theory, but conformity and compromise in practice.

Students in most academic programs are bred to be partners of the system, not to challenge it. It is part of the nature of institutions in our time. Whether the issue be social justice, peace, public health, poverty, or the environment, all make candidates for study, research, statistics, coursework, documentation, literature, and professional careers, while the poor remain impoverished, environmental quality worsens, and our last remaining shreds of wild, original America are placed in increasing peril.

Martin Luther King, Jr. saw three major evils – racism, poverty, and militarism – and found them integrally linked, one with the other. I see the degraded environment as a fourth major evil, also joined with the others. Environmentalists speak of concern with forests, water, air, soil, fish and wildlife, land use, and use of resources, but these are only symptoms of a sick society that needs to deal more fundamentally with itself. Presidents and Congresses, one after another, Democratic as well as Republican, have opposed anything but the most niggardly expenditures to educate and house the poor, provide for the aging, rehabilitate the imprisoned and the mentally ill; in the very same fashion they cannot find funds to protect the soil, safeguard the wilderness, or enhance wildlife. The United States has spent vast sums for so-called security from other nations, while for a fraction of that amount it could have extended humanitarian aid and eliminated the threat of war.

These official actions reflect a system that places a low priority on human values and natural values, a system that needs to reorder priorities while there is still the chance. The compartmentalized approach to life marks the late twentieth century, but the truth is we are all connected. Living that truth begins by recognizing that every human being is rightfully entitled to housing, work, health care, proper nutrition, an adequate income in a habitable environment, and a world at peace.

I find myself turning increasingly to the state of things beyond the wilderness. The nature reserve cannot be decoupled from the society around it. Now I must consider that in the past ten years the population of our prisons has doubled, that we put more people in our prisons than any other "advanced" country, except South Africa and the Soviet Union, and that we have the highest crime rate. Prisons are overcrowded and notoriously inhumane. Most of those found guilty of crimes against society are themselves the victims of society. By this I mean that prison inmates early in their lives suffered child abuse, incest, brutality, and poverty. The poor and uneducated, society's disenfranchised, feel the fury of the justice system, assigned to the worst conditions and the longest terms, while the insiders, like Ivan Boesky and Lynn Nofziger, guilty of connivance, corruption, and theft, get off lightly, serving short sentences in country club prisons.

In the last eight years, the proportion of nonmilitary spending has been reduced by eight percent, while military spending has more than doubled. With the United States in the lead, the world spends $1.7 million per minute on military forces and equipment – $800 billion per year – or $30,000 per soldier, as compared with $455 per child for education. The United States ranks thirteenth among nations in infant mortality, ninth in literacy, and first in weapons production.

Something is wrong, critically wrong. A society that produces beggars needs restructuring. Martin Luther King, Jr. spoke of the need for compassion. True compassion, he said, involves more than flinging a coin to a beggar. It is not haphazard and superficial. A true revolution of values soon will look uneasily on the glaring contrast of poverty and wealth.

Natural resource professionals ought to be in the lead of the revolution of values. So should the environmental organizations and the people working for them. The problem is that compassion must be at the root of the revolution of values, while compassion, and emotion, are repressed in the training of natural resource professionals and obscured in the management of organizations. Earlier this year I spoke at an environmental conference in Alaska, after which I received a letter from one of the participants. She wrote as follows: "Not once in the ten years I spent studying forestry and land management while getting the Ph.D. did anyone ever speak about ethics."

I am not sure they speak much about ethics in the training of environmental professionals either. Thirty years ago, saving the earth was a mission rather than a career. The spirit of the earlier, pre-World War II leaders pervaded the environmental movement, among them Aldo Leopold and Jay "Ding" Darling in the wildlife field; Bob Marshall and Robert Sterling Yard in wilderness and national parks; and Will Dilg, who sparked the organization of the Izaak Walton League. Thirty years ago they were personally remembered and spoken of by those who knew them; Olaus Murie, Benton MacKaye, and Arthur Carhart were still alive. Organizations were led by self-sacrificing missionaries and zealots like Howard Zahniser of the Wilderness Society; Joe Penfold of the Izaak Walton League; Fred Packard and Devereux Butcher of the National Parks Association; and the "archdruid," David Brower of the Sierra Club. Some of their directors, like

Sigurd Olson and Harvey Broome, were cut from the same cloth. Broome was a particular friend of mine, a successful lawyer in Knoxville, Tennessee, who gave up his practice to become a law clerk to a judge, with the understanding that he could take time off as needed to pursue his primary interest in wilderness preservation, as a member of the governing council and president of the Wilderness Society.

Now, people go to some very respectable colleges and universities to train for professional careers in the environment. My own daughter attended Williams College and the Kennedy School of Government at Harvard, which I suppose qualifies her for the position she now holds with the Environmental Law Institute. But I am not sure that she experienced the ethical cause of the poor and disenfranchised relative to a healthy environment.

During the sixties and seventies, I observed an abundance of environmental reforms, but reforms are all they proved to be, rather like masking the corpse. In the sixties the Interior Department was busy promoting the establishment of new national parks, which environmentalists cheered, while at the same time underwriting massive power plants in the Southwest, degrading the air quality of the Grand Canyon and other national parks of the region. Interior Secretary Stewart Udall spoke of the good that would come to Hopi and Navajo Indians from exploitation of "their underutilized coal resources," without reference to the inevitable polluted air to which the Indians would be subjected and, even worse, their displacement to make way for strip mining of those "underutilized" resources.

Strip mining was a major issue in the sixties and seventies. Activists in the coal country fought to stop it altogether as heedless destruction of natural and human resources. So did Ken Hechler, a West Virginia scholar in Congress, who pursued principle above political expediency. He insisted that if environmentalists held firm and lobbied hard, they would win. National leaders, however, felt the odds were too long; the best that could be attained was legislation to control the practice of strip mining. Thus, I recall being at the White House when President Jimmy Carter ceremoniously signed the new strip mining law. Jubilation prevailed over the prospect of a bright beginning in the coal fields. Essentially, however, that new law legitimized strip mining, establishing standards and a new bureaucracy to enforce them, as best it could, or would, leaving the local activists bitter and disappointed.

The same scenario, with variation, was written in dealing with clearcutting in the national forests. A court decision in the case of the Monongahela National Forest (in West Virginia), based on forest legislation of 1897, was widely interpreted as halting all logging on all national forests, though selective logging was still wholly within bounds. In the lobbying confrontations of the 1970s, national environmental leaders, fearing the political power of the timber-forestry coalition, opted to accept new systems of planning via the Forest and Range Renewable Resources Planning Act of 1974 and the National Forest Management Act of 1976, both of which established standards and processes, without seriously curbing clearcutting or reducing the volume of timber removed from the national forests.

Paper victories are tough enough to come by, but they create illusions rather than effective environmental progress. One added illustration involves the national parks. A particular superintendent was assigned by his superiors to prepare a wilderness proposal for his park. The regional director admonished him to leave out two politically controversial portions. "Then," said the director, "we should have no difficulty in getting it through Congress." But the superintendent refused, recalling later, "I was more concerned with saving the wilderness than in getting a law-passed saying that I had done so."

Gifford Pinchot may have said it best. In 1910, when forestry was a vital, progressive force in the forefront of the conservation crusade, he wrote:

> We have allowed the great corporations to occupy with their own men the strategic points in business, in social and political life. It is our fault more than theirs. We have allowed it when we could have stopped it. Too often we have seemed to forget that a man in public life can no more serve both the special interests and the people than he can serve God and Mammon. There is no reason why the American people should not take into their hands again the full political power which is theirs by right, and which they exercised before the special interests began to nullify the will of the majority.

The desire for a more environmentally-based society has become deeply rooted since the sixties. The public has shown a high level of support for environmental protection. Despite energy shortages in the seventies, recessions, the cost of environmental laws, and Reagan landslides, a variety of surveys shows little evidence that the public wants to reduce environmental protection programs by less regulation or less spending. Given the choice, a majority favors less economic growth. Surveys consistently indicate that people feel protecting the environment is more important than keeping prices down on products they buy.

However, something new must be done by a new group of people. The priority item on the agenda, as I see it, is for those who hope to heal the earth to join with those who hope to heal the souls of our fellows to bring something new to bear. We must face the twenty-first century with new emphasis on human care and concern. A fair profit may be defensible, but profiteering has skyrocketed at the expense of social and environmental responsibility. The proposal to open the Arctic National Wildlife Refuge to oil exploration and drilling offers a classic case in point: It does not have a damn thing to do with meeting human needs. Profiteering should never be glorified, nor confused with social services.

We cannot set aside a little bit of wilderness and say, "That much will take care of the soul side of America." We must rescue everything that still remains wild and recapture a lot more that has been lost, looking to its future rather than its past. In the battle for wilderness there are no enemies. The children of the poor will become rich for what is saved; the children of the rich will be impoverished for what is not saved. It takes considerable courage to stand up against money and the power of politics and institutions. It takes wisdom, or at least knowledge and courage, to work through the system. When the Pope visited the United States he said, "We need more than social reformers; we need saints." I would say, "We need more than social reformers; we need revolutionaries – not to commit violent acts but to press society to reorder its priorities."

"New opinions are always suspected, and usually opposed," wrote John Locke more than three centuries ago, "without any other reason but because they are not already common." Such is the way of institutions, but not of individuals. Only the individualist can succeed, even in our age of stereotypes, for true success comes only from within. When we look at the revolutionary task of reordering priorities, and the sheer power of entrenched, interlocked institutions, the challenge may seem utterly impossible. Yet, individuals working together, or even alone, at the grass-roots of America, have worked miracles. The odds in Selma and Montgomery, Alabama, also looked impossible, in the long fight for the Wilderness Act, and for Overton Park and many other places like it.

"A nation that continues year after year to spend more money on military defense than on programs of social uplift is approaching spiritual death," wrote Martin Luther King, Jr. who embodied in his own self the challenge to spiritual life. Each individual must realize the power of his and her own life and never sell it short. In setting the agenda for tomorrow, miracles large and small are within reach.

A chapter in *Crossroads: Environmental Priorities for the Future*, Peter Borelli, editor, 1988.

20. Writer with a cause:
Richard Neuberger

"When is a bribe not a bribe?

"That's easy. When the money is a campaign contribution!"

Richard L. Neuberger asked the question and gave the irrefutable answer more than forty years ago, though it is just as valid and applicable today. He was a politician, and proud of it, but really a journalist first, and a conservationist, one of the finest in the history of the Northwest. It's time and timely, I say, to relearn who he was and what he stood for, and to rekindle the Neuberger spirit into public affairs.

When he ran to represent Oregon in the United States Senate, Neuberger didn't want to use a teleprompter or "idiot boards" on television. "Let's tell the people you don't play like that," reasoned his wife, partner and best friend, Maurine. They would start campaigning at 6 a.m, speak in locomotive roundhouses, share chuck wagon meals with cowpunchers and talk with Indians at the edge of the Columbia River rapids, without stopping until midnight.

At first, because they had no funds, they traveled by themselves, without entourage, or even a single aide or consultant. Later, when funding became available, they still traveled that way – for they found that Oregon's people took to a husband-and-wife out on their own much better than to the elaborate retinue of advertising counselors, press agents, and politicians that convoyed his opponent, the incumbent, Guy Cordon.

Neuberger won the election, breaking a Republican monopoly in Oregon politics. When he went to Washington in 1954 as a member of the U.S. Senate, he brought with him a strong conservation platform based on opposition to the giveaway policies of the Eisenhower administration, and he lived it out to the hilt, until his death, six years later.

Talking conservation on the political stage was different in those days. Maurine Neuberger a few years ago reminded me of a high official who referred to "birdwatchers" with a slur in his voice. And when Dick made a plea on the Senate floor for preserving the endangered whooping crane and told the story of the passage of the last carrier pigeon, critical insiders considered it almost laughable, beneath the behavior expected of a United States senator.

The Neubergers were involved with the environment from the time they were married in 1945. Even before World War II he had already established himself as the foremost media interpreter of environmental issues in the Northwest, contributing regularly to the *New York Times* and diverse national magazines. He grew from an observer of politics into a participant, first as a member of the Oregon House of Representatives in 1941 at age 27, then, after returning from military duty, the State Senate in 1949.

When Maurine was elected to the lower house they made a formidable legislative team, crusading to save Oregon's vaunted natural scenery from the unnatural blight of billboards along the highways. They took that issue, among others, to Washington with them. Dick, albeit a freshman in the Senate, insisted on including billboard control in federal highway legislation, refusing to be browbeaten by Robert F. Kerr, of Oklahoma, the powerful oil mogul and big business apostle. The Neubergers had already been through all the arguments and political pressures at home and knew that billboards would be worth nothing if government did not build the highways.

While in Washington, Dick Neuberger was "Mr. Conservation," associated with every positive piece of environmental legislation. He was responsible for establishment of Fort Clatsop National Historic Park and Oregon Dunes National Recreation Area in his own state and he helped make the country conscious of the marvel called Hells Canyon on the Snake River. His finest hours in my book came as co-sponsor, with Sen. Hubert Humphrey, of Minnesota, of the Wilderness Bill. At the first committee hearings in 1957, Neuberger spoke eloquently, tolling the bell at "the eleventh hour" for saving the nation's wilderness heritage. He told of the great forests of the Northwest. "If only such magnificent trees could last forever," he said. "But are we letting commercialization and exploitation rob us of our chance for unfettered enjoyment under the blue heavens and the stars?"

Then he added:

> I know that millions of Americans feel likewise. They gain both security and comfort from the fact that a segment of the old original wilderness has been saved. The whole continent has not yet been tilled, paved or settled. Some of these people may never see the real wilderness:

their sentiments are purely vicarious. But they are aware of it nevertheless – just as Mount Everest and K-2 inspire pride among people in
remote parts of India.

Maurine, for her part, worked as an unpaid staff member, doing leg-
work and research, attending hearings on the Wilderness Act, writing the
newsletter for home constituents, standing in at social functions. She also
did research for her husband as a journalist and author. Following his
death, she succeeded him for one term in the Senate in her own right and
is still a great lady at home in Portland.

"He had singleness of purpose as a writer," she once told me. "He was
not terribly social. He disliked a lot of Washington social life and would
rather write. Friends and editors marveled that he could be a United States
senator and still contribute to magazines like *Saturday Evening Post* and
Harper's, but it gave him more pleasure to see his name in a magazine as
author of an article than to read something about himself. He had a gift of
expression that made him effective on the Senate floor, but he was looking forward to returning home to Portland, to write."

Neuberger himself wondered whether he belonged in politics. "Say
nothing, and say it well," he was advised by an older U.S. senator interested in Neuberger's budding career. He wondered whether it was proper
to mix his craft as a writer with political office. But he said, "When I see
Oregon's teachers paid the lowest salaries on the Coast, when I see a private utility company selling the power from the dam at Bonneville which
the people built and paid for, when I see a Japanese-American soldier with
forty-one blood transfusions denied a hotel room on a rainy night, when I
see a million-dollar race track rising while veterans cannot construct
homes – then my blood pressure rises too, and I wonder if any case is
strong enough to impel abdication in favor of those who tolerate these
things."

When he learned in 1959 that he had cancer, he wrote about that, too:
"I realize, finally, that I am not immortal. I shudder when 1 remember all
the occasions that I spoiled for myself, even when I was in the best of
health – by false pride, synthetic values and fancied slights."

He changed politically, too, declaring that he could never again be
wholly partisan. I doubt, however, that he ever really was. He was never
stubborn or bull-headed. He believed in democratic process and loved the
Senate. The best advice he ever received was to recognize "the other fellow may be right."

Thus, response to the news of his cancer reflected no party lines. Republicans in Oregon offered to give blood if a transfusion was necessary. Senator Barry Goldwater and his wife said they were praying for him. Republican senators called at his office to inquire after his health (while Democratic liberal colleagues went unheard from).

Richard Neuberger passed on to his reward in 1960. He was only forty-seven, his best contributions to politics, journalism and the environment most likely still ahead. Fortunately, he left a legacy in his writing, with some of the best pieces assembled in *They Never Go Back to Pocatello*, published (in 1988) by the Oregon Historical Society, with foreword by Maurine Neuberger and biographical information by Steve Neal. It's a great work – I find something special on every page, with messages for today and tomorrow.

It includes his first major article, "The New Germany," which he wrote for *The Nation* in 1933, when he was twenty-one. He had just been to Europe, observing Hitler's rise to power, and thus warned that "no one who looks behind the barrier of censorship and deceit in Germany can doubt that one of the major premises of the Nazi movement is intense preparation for a war of aggression."

In "The Tyranny of Guilt by Association," published in *The Progressive* in 1955, he noted that he was sometimes accused of radicalism because he wrote for the *New Republic, Nation,* and *The Progressive* – yet there was no "innocence by association" and few ever suggested that his substantial writing for "conservative" magazines like *Reader's Digest* and *Saturday Evening Post* make him a conservative.

For all his experience and opportunities elsewhere, he was always a Northwesterner, specifically a Portlander, at heart. In "My Hometown is Good Enough for Me," which appeared in the *Saturday Evening Post* in 1950, he wrote: "When I look out across the slanting ramparts of the Cascades to Hood's frosty peak, I feel like Antaeus, the mythical giant who gained strength merely by touching the earth. This is my own special corner of my native land. This is where my bearded grandfather came from the Old World in 1870, even ahead of the railroads."

I never met Dick Neuberger personally. However, on Feb. 15, 1959, *Parade Magazine*, the Sunday supplement, published an article of mine, "What's Happening to Our Shoreline?" Two days later Senator Neuberger introduced the article in the Congressional Record. There was nothing unusual about that – congressmen load the appendix to the Record with all kinds of relevancies and irrelevancies – but Neuberger was a man I much admired as a writer with a cause who made his mark in public life.

Moreover, in his remarks Senator Neuberger said he was introducing the article in tribute to a former Oregon governor, Oswald West, who still lived in retirement in Portland at the age of 85. The point was that Oswald West, as governor from 1911 to 1915, kept one of the most beautiful seacoasts on earth from being exploited for private gain and greed. He saw to it that the law of riparian rights safeguarded the 300-mile coast for perpetual public benefit, rather than permitting it to be devoured for commercial uses.

"That this shore of white sandy beaches and timbered headlands has not been defiled or looted," Senator Neuberger wrote, "is due to the foresight, vision and courage of ex-Governor Oswald West." I was struck then, and have been over and over ever since, with the abundant individual opportunity to serve the public good through foresight, vision and courage. And that is the legacy, the gift in spirit, left by Richard Neuberger.

Cascadia Times, 1997.

21. He dignified the scene:
an obit for John Oakes

John B. Oakes, the legendary editorial page editor of the *New York Times* in the sixties and seventies, died in April 2001 at the age of 87. Oakes had joined the *Times* in 1946 after serving in the military during World War II and four years as a political reporter at the *Washington Post*. He was a valedictorian at Princeton University and a Rhodes scholar.

His job at the *Times* initially was editor of the Review of the Week section. As a sideline during the 1950s he wrote a Sunday column, "Conservation," expressing his lifelong concern for the environment. In the edition of May 13, 1956 his conservation column commended new legislation introduced by Senator Hubert Humphrey to establish a national wilderness preservation system. It was the beginning of the long political fight leading to passage of the Wilderness Act of 1964.

During the fifteen years, starting in 1961, he ran the editorial page, Oakes editorialized about civil rights, the presidency, foreign affairs, politics and the environment, defining a lofty agenda of public policy. When he retired, his colleagues paid editorial homage (on January 1, 1977):

> He could not and would not prettify the scene. But he dignified it, with a conscientiousness and with standards that were unyielding and with a boundless confidence that if only sound values and solid information could be located in the confusion of events, the citizen reader would distinguish the right from the wrong and uphold the public good.

Even after retirement Oakes contributed powerful opinion pieces to the Op-Ed page (which he had started in 1970), including "Watt's Very Wrong," December 31, 1980, when James G. Watt's nomination was pending in the Senate; "Japan, Swallow Hard and Stop Whaling," January 19, 1983; and "Adirondack SOS," October 29, 1988 (which elicited a letter to the editor of the *Times* from Governor Mario Cuomo pledging renewed commitment to preserving the Adirondacks). In correspondence with me, he discussed the memoir written by Katherine Graham, publisher of the *Washington Post*, in which Oakes was mentioned. He wrote as follows:

> The 'house' you referred to began with a group of some six or eight bachelors (mostly fresh out of Harvard or Yale law school) at 1913 S Street. After a year or so, some of us moved across the [Potomac] river to a larger house (called 'Hockley') in Arlington, where our number grew to some ten or twelve. In 1941, after several of us had entered Army or Navy, the 'house' continued on Foxhall Road.
>
> You asked about Kay Graham. She and I were both reporters at the *Washington Post* and I brought her out to our occasional cocktail parties, where she first met Phil Graham [whom she later married]. You also mentioned Henry Reuss, who joined us after we had moved from S Street to Hockley – and who not only became a very distinguished congressman from Wisconsin but a fine conservationist too.

John Oakes received many awards for his environmental work and served at various times on the boards of the National Parks and Conservation Association, Natural Resources Defense Council and the Wilderness Society.

> Written for *E-Streeter*, newsletter of Washington Post alumni who worked in the old plant, 2001

* * * * * *

A few additional words about John Oakes are in order here. Robert Bendiner, a colleague of his, wrote in retrospect that Oakes was a sober man of firm convictions held in place by a consistent will and conveyed by clear serious prose. I don't doubt he could be seriously sober in sticking to principles while defining editorial content; after all, those editorials in the *Times* have been cited the world over. But I think there was a cheery, smiling side to him. I remember he mentioned to me introducing to the editorial page the poetry of a well known nature writer and yet lamenting wistfully that he was allowed to pay only a minimum rate for it.

Once we discussed at length the matter of objectivity in news reporting. He disagreed with my view that there is no such thing as objectivity:

> I was brought up in the tradition of objective reporting and still believe that news stories ought to be as objective and non-editorial as

humanly possible. Pieces that express the opinion of the writer should be reserved for specially marked magazine pieces and, of course, editorials. I have found myself saying more than once about a given story, I'm delighted to see this, but it should have been a news analysis, or editorial, or op-ed piece or something else. Let the facts speak for themselves, that's the way it ought to be. The public ought to be free to make up its own mind.

I certainly respect his view. For a time, while he was still alive, I thought I would like to write a biography about him. Now perhaps the best I can do is hope that some serious historian will put together a selection of John B. Oakes' classy editorials from pages of the *New York Times*.

22. Reaffirming the writer's role

When I joined the protest against the World Trade Organization in Seattle in late 1999, I felt as though listening to a wakeup call, a challenge to professionals to rethink our place in modern society, to reconsider what we do, what we buy, what we don't buy, and how we conduct our lives personally and professionally. Since then, I've thought especially about the appropriate response of writers to the globalization of trade and to the outcries against it.

Pundits of the mainstream media tossed verbal brickbats, determined to trivialize the Seattle protest. They kept insisting that free trade benefits the poor, makes jobs and opens markets, and that poor nations suffer from protectionism in the USA. But that doesn't add up – not when children work in the worst sweatshops on earth instead of going to school, when unionists are arrested, fired and killed, and when writers speaking for them suffer the same fate.

Mainstream media focused on the isolated incidents of violence in Seattle. They ignored educational forums conducted by religious and peace groups about Jubilee 2000, the program of debt forgiveness for the poorest nations on earth. But then the mass media themselves, the frontline messengers of consumerism and infinite growth, are part of the problem, hardly of the solution.

Journalists and authors tend to consider themselves compromised intellectually by involvement and activism, but freedom of expression is clearly restricted by the power and influence of corporate rule. A handful of mammoth private organizations (Disney, Time Warner, Bertelsmann, Rupert Murdoch, Hachette and Viacom) dominate the mass media, controlling the world's news gathering, current affairs, entertainment and publishing. They define social and cultural attitudes. They shape public images of political leaders and political debate. They squeeze writers with book contracts demanding that we work for less, that we surrender all rights, and carry our own liability insurance.

Television is the worst. It distorts reality, keeps people indoors, validates noise over quiet, entertainment over dialogue. Most of it, whether comedy, drama or documentary, is mediocre and mind numbing. Sometimes I wonder about the TV writers and what they really wanted to do at the start of their careers.

These media giants are globalized. They want free trade, free to enter any country and dominate its periodicals, television, films, music and videos with messages of materialism and consumerism at the very time when worldviews of the West should be challenged

But, of course, writing is a business and business is about money. Or so I might believe after reading the program of the twenty-ninth annual writers conference conducted by the American Society of Journalists and Authors in April 2000. The theme of the conference was "selling your work in the 2000s." Consistent with it were seminars titled "Book Proposals that Sell"; "There's Great Money in Writing for Good Magazines"; "Cashing in Online – How to Earn Top Pay from the Biggest Sites," and "Hot New Book Revolution: E-, On-Demand, and Internet Publishing." I could have learned to make it on the money trail by writing about spirituality because it's "this fast-growing field" and if I could not be sufficiently spiritual, then I could go for "Big Money: Business and Corporate Writing" or for single-sponsor publications and their "New Opportunities in Advertorials, Magazines, Newsletters."

It isn't only ASJA that encourages writers to write corporate. *A Field Guide for Science Writers*, a whole book featuring essays by thirty-plus members of the National Association of Science Writers, shows science writing heavily influenced and employed by corporations, trade associations, educational institutions, and government agencies. Apparently there's plenty of work and money in preparing press releases, news and feature stories for magazines, speeches, radio and television reports, and research magazines, newsletters, newspapers and brochures. The federal government alone spends $40 billion a year on civilian science and technology programs, plus another $30 billion on military research and development. That is why many of these agencies hire science writers – as full-time employees and free-lancers on assignment – to get the message out and convince the taxpaying public that all is well.

The trouble is that allegiance of the science writers-for-hire belongs to the institution that employs them, even when work is denatured for politics rather than science. Or, as Rick E. Borchelt, special assistant for public affairs at the White House, a member of the board of the National Association of Science Writers, explains in the *Field Guide*: "The first rule in coping with agency editing is never to get personally interested in anything you write. Nine times out of ten you may not recognize it when it comes out of review."

Maybe science writers, and education writers too, should know about the readiness of corporations to provide teaching kits, activity books, readings, and quizzes for use in the classrooms of the country. Somebody, after all, was paid to write the script of the classroom video, *Scientists and the Alaska Oil Spill*, showing that Exxon's Valdez oil spill really wasn't bad; the materials proving that increased carbon dioxide induced by global warming makes plants grow larger; cutting down mature trees promotes the growth of forests, and the great line, "The quality and abundance of our food supply is due to modern agricultural practices, which include the use of pesticides."

The American Poultry Association, National Hot Dog and Sausage Council, California Beef Council, American Egg Board, and National Livestock and Meat Board all hire writers to produce classroom materials – like the Meat Board's science kit that teaches being short is the result of eating too little meat. The National Potato Board and Snack Food Association, representing the same corporations that advertise junk food on television, offer an absolutely free educational program, *Count Your Chips*, focusing on math, social science and language arts. It includes researching people's favorite chip flavors and writing a "humorous family snack story."

No thanks, I say. We need to raise children with a better set of values, treating the earth and its creatures with respect, care and justice. And no thanks again, to the writers organization that identifies with that kind of writing. Yes, I've heard many times over the warning: "Don't let writing obscure your business vision." But I prefer to say: "Don't let business obscure your writing goal."

I.F. Stone in his illustrious career exemplified principle above expediency. As he wrote on closing shop in 1971 after nineteen heroic years of *I.F. Stone's Weekly*:

> To give a little comfort to the oppressed, to write the truth exactly as I saw it, to make no compromise other than those of quality imposed by my own inadequacies, to be free to follow no master other than my own

compulsions, to live up to my idealized image of what a true newspaper-man should be, and still be able to make a living for my family – what more could a man ask?

Rachel Carson was that way, too. When she saw the wholesale destruction of wildlife and its habitat consequent to the use of DDT and other toxic poisons, she committed herself to write the manuscript that became *Silent Spring*. The choice was simple: "I have felt bound by a solemn obligation to do what I could – if I didn't at least try I could never again be happy in nature."

Maybe William Faulkner said it best. In accepting the 1950 Nobel Prize for Literature, he declared:

> The young man or woman writing today has forgotten the problems of the human heart in conflict with itself which alone can make good writing because only that is worth writing about, worth the agony and the sweat. He must learn them again. He must teach himself that the basest of all things is to be afraid. It is his privilege to help man endure by lifting his heart, by reminding him of the courage and honor and hope and pride and compassion and pity and sacrifice which have been the glory of his past.

It isn't easy, certainly it wasn't easy for Carson, Faulkner or Stone, but I believe that in our democratic society avenues of communication will always be open, and that each of us must be inspired to realize the power of his or her own life and never sell it short. True enough, top-flight magazines like the *Saturday Evening Post, Collier's, True*, and *Holiday* have disappeared. Newspapers have folded and declined. But new breeds of media are rising all across America to fill the gaps of social concern and critical commentary the mainstream has avoided.

Maine Times is one of them, with a philosophy that proves it worthwhile. As Peter W. Cox editorialized in the issue of July 15, 1994:

> To a public nurtured on 'infotainment,' any serious writing is boring. The vast majority of Americans do not read for intellectual stimulation, with the result that the best-written literary novel is lucky to sell 10,000 copies nationwide. Thrillers, yes. A new Faulkner, forget it.
>
> For years, the daily press tried to dumb down its stories, to make them shorter and less complex. I always felt the result was that they did not gain the non-reader; they simply lost the involved citizen. I always

accepted the fact that most people bought a daily paper for the sports scores, the comics and the TV listings.

Should *Maine Times* be difficult for an uninformed person to read? Yes, there is no way around it. But *Maine Times* should also offer the person the opportunity to become truly informed. For me, the worst result would be a "successful" *Maine Times* that is irrelevant to the future of Maine.

Personally, I think I would measure success by getting published in *Maine Times* and if not there then in something like it that sets its standards high, even though it may pay less.

The same principle applies to books. In the Winter 2000 issue of the *Authors Guild Bulletin*, Guild president Letty Cottin Pogrebin, reported on "two years of exhaustive research, discussion and revision" detailing the declining status of "midlist books." But it's all relative. I suspect the Guild's midlist looks puny only in comparison to the "blockbusters" the corporate giants hold dear. On the other hand, smaller publishers and university presses are likely to regard the same midlist books as toplist. My own experience has shown those presses run by competent people who care, about the quality of books and about their authors. Faulkner would be welcome.

They sell books too, maybe not in the same volume, but enough to matter, and new publishing houses keep coming along. For example, the Hub City Writers Project, a cooperative group in Spartanburg, South Carolina, has published nine books since it began in 1995. These include *The Seasons of Harold Hatcher*, by a South Carolina writer, Mike Hembree, a beautiful story about a man of simple ways who created a community garden and woodland preserve, in the process changing lives and the way the city sees itself. Harold Hatcher has never owned a credit card, but at 92 or 93 still works in the garden, working for an ecological, ethical future.

It may appear difficult to factor such a simple story into a response to the globalization of trade, but maybe that is where it begins. It impresses me as part of the wakeup call, a challenge to rethink our place in modern society, to reconsider what we do, what we buy, what we don't buy, and how we conduct our lives personally and professionally.

Newsletter of the American Society of Journalists and Authors, 2000.

23. Illusions of objectivity

One day in class a student, Heather, raised her hand to speak. Her eyes were bright with a revelation. "There is a difference," she announced, "between covering the environment and environmental journalism."

Heather was absolutely correct. Environmental journalism requires learning more than "how to write," but learning the power of emotion and imagery, to think not simply of Who, What, Where, When and How, but to think Whole, with breadth, depth, perspective and feeling.

This is not the way it works in mainstream or conventional journalism, which continues to suffer under the illusion and delusion that "objectivity" actually prevails in newspapers, radio and television and that journalists must set aside personal feeling for their subjects or get out.

"There is no dispassionate objectivity" wrote Saul Alinsky in *Rules for Radicals*. That has been said and shown in a thousand different ways. Business news is almost always interpreted from the business viewpoint. So are sports, food, automotive, aviation, travel and real estate news. Public relations, the spin doctors working for powerful corporate and government interests, constitute a preeminent influence on how news is covered and presented. But then the media themselves are corporate, driven far more by profit than public service.

Commercial television is probably worst of all, mind numbing, dumbing down America, fostering the gospel of an over-consumptive, wasteful age. Nevertheless, "advocacy" is a word journalists have been taught to avoid, presumably because it marks a bias, something that should not be acknowledged. But we ought to be advocates for the health and safety of the planet, concerned with global warming, acid rain, destruction of tropical and temperate forests, toxic wastes, pollution of air and water, and population pressures that degrade the quality of life.

Moreover, the world we live in is divided between those who do not have enough and those who have more than enough. It grieves me that the United States should lead in widening the gap between the underprivileged

– the homeless, hungry and hopeless – and the overprivileged who want still more. Clearly it is time to ask for new and better answers.

That is what journalism is meant to do. The late I.F. Stone said he wanted only to live up to his "idealized image of what a true newspaperman should be." I've always felt the same way while taking my share of lumps.

Thus I could empathize with Stone, who followed a lonely road in Washington while publishing his investigative and political newsletter. In 1941 he was expelled from the National Press Club for bringing a black judge as his lunch guest. He was hounded by the FBI, excoriated on the floor of Congress, and scorned by colleagues of the media. When he closed shop in December 1971, Stone wrote:

> The place to be is where the odds are against you; power breeds injustice, and to defend the underdog against the triumphant is more exhilarating than to curry favor and move safely with the mob. Philosophically I believe a man's life reduces itself ultimately to a faith – the fundamental is beyond proof – and that faith is a matter of aesthetics, a sense of beauty and harmony. I think every man is his own Pygmalion, and spends his life fashioning himself. And in fashioning himself, for good or evil, he fashions the human race and its future.

Pursuing the concept of faith and aesthetics, of beauty and harmony, coupled with the essential element of ethics, is fundamental to a fulfilling career. Albert Schweitzer taught that a person is ethical when life becomes sacred, not simply his or her own life, but that of all humans, and of plants and animals, and when he or she devotes himself or herself to other living things. That commitment is implicit in environmental journalism.

Schweitzer followed the creed of Ralph Waldo Emerson, who insisted that "literature, poetry and science are all homage of man to the unfathomed secrets of nature," that all things are friendly and sacred, all days holy, all beings divine, and that every animal in its growth teaches unity of cause.

And Thomas Merton wrote that he discovered new perceptions of ethics once he was free of a society falsely happy because it felt protected by military might, a society imaged in the mass media, advertising, movies, television, and best sellers, "pompous and trifling masks that hide hypocrisy, cruelty and fear."

Rachel Carson wanted to tell the story of pesticides through one magazine or another, but none would have it. Once she published *Silent Spring*, most of the media ridiculed it, parroting chemical industry propaganda. Ultimately she reviewed and defined her goal:

> The beauty of the living world I was trying to save has always been uppermost in my mind – that, and anger at the senseless brutish things that were being done. I have felt bound by a solemn obligation to do what I could – if I didn't at least try I could never again be happy in nature.

For myself, I see imagination and a subjective value system as a force empowering the individual who cares and desires to rise above sheer facts, which may not be so factual after all. To say it another way, the source of strength in human life is in emotion, reverence and passion, for the earth and its human web of life. I didn't think this up. It's an old, ancient idea.

But modern society is obsessed with facts and figures, with modern machinery providing access to even more numbers. Alas, the analytical type of thinking of western civilization has given us the power over nature yet smothered us in ignorance about ourselves as part of it.

In other words, individuals succeed when they rise above themselves, and above institutions, to challenge an entrenched system in which a small minority controls wealth and power. There must be serious commitment, risk-taking, personal self-sacrifice. Most of those willing to sacrifice never do it for salaries; yet crusades for social issues, whether for peace, racial equality, gender rights, or the environment, show how people – at times a very few – can and do bring needed change. The effort itself is rewarding, more than any success the effort may bring.

I recognize that mine is not the most popular or accepted approach – and definitely not in the ranks of the Society of Environmental Journalists. The SEJ presumes to "advance public understanding of environmental issues by improving the quality, accuracy and visibility of environmental reporting," but is influenced largely by mainstream, tradition-bound reporters. In an article in the media watchdog magazine, *EXTRA!* (January-February 1997), titled "Saving the Earth Isn't Their Job: Rachel Carson Wouldn't Recognize Many Environmental Journalists Today," Karl Grossman wrote that much of the SEJ "has a problem with investigative journalism – or anything else that could be labeled 'advocacy.'"

Grossman related his experience of attending a conference to consider the organization's future direction. Noel Grove, editor of the *SEJournal*, asked conference attendees about printing on 100 percent recycled paper.

"That would be advocacy!" came a chorus in reply. Grove got the message: A note in the Fall 1998 SEJournal announced that "the former Green Beat," a section designed as an idea exchange for environmental journalists and editors – "has been changed to The Beat to avoid any appearance of bias in the *SEJournal*."

At times, now and then, mainstream journalists are allowed to demonstrate their bias and to do wonderful work. Dick Smith joined the staff of the *Santa Barbara News Press* in 1948 and made the backcountry of the Los Padres National Forest his special beat, roaming the trails and canyons with camera and notebook. He was the untiring guardian of wilderness, "the conscience of the county." He studied the California condor and helped gain recognition of it as a species in need of special protection. Smith sparked the effort to designate the San Rafael Wilderness, the first one reviewed by Congress and set aside under the 1964 Wilderness Act, and wanted a large adjacent area added to it. When he died suddenly in 1977, the mayor proclaimed Dick Smith Week and the whole city mourned. All kinds of groups and officials supported the wilderness extension, which became the Dick Smith Wilderness.

This country and the world need more Dick Smiths to stir the public conscience with diligent research, reporting and writing on critical environmental issues. An article about the humongous Three Gorges Dam in China by Wu Mei in the Winter 1999 issue of the *Media Studies Journal* reveals that from 1984 to 1989, when the megaproject was hotly debated in the inner circle of the Chinese government and engineering consortiums, when government agencies in both the United States and Canada were either seeking contracts or providing feasibility studies, American coverage of the megadam was superficial. The Three Gorges dam was never a big "story" in major newspapers.

Well, it ought to be a big story. Whether it's the Three Gorges in China or the environmental challenges in our own communities, the big stories will be when journalists and their editors courageously and shamelessly show that they care about humanity and the earth.

Montana Journalism Review, 1999.

24. Sacred space, Sacred power

The first time I read about the Wilderness Act – or the Wilderness Bill at that time – was in the *New York Times* of May 15, 1956. In the column headed "Conservation," John B. Oakes reported that Senator Hubert Humphrey, of Minnesota, was sponsoring legislation to establish a national wilderness preservation system. "The idea is certainly worth exploring," Oakes wrote, "if what is left of our country in a natural state is worth saving, as many of us believe it is." Oakes outlined the problem as follows:

> This isn't just a question of city folks seeking outdoor recreation, or enjoying spectacular scenery, or breathing unpoisoned air. It goes much deeper; it springs from the inextricable relationship of man with nature, a relationship that even the most insensitive and complex civilization can never dissipate. Man needs nature; he may within limits control it, but to destroy it is to begin the destruction of man himself. We cannot live on a sterile planet, nor would we want to.

John Oakes stirred my conscience, and my curiosity to learn more. I determined in due course that he was voicing a viewpoint deeply rooted in American culture and history, manifest in earlier days through the works of William Bartrem, James Fenimore Cooper, William Cullen Bryant, John J. Audubon, Ralph Waldo Emerson, Henry David Thoreau and John Muir. Muir felt uplifted and exalted in the wild sanctuary: Wilderness to him was an expression of God on earth – the mountains, God's temples; the forests, sacred groves. In our own age the idea was expressed by Ansel Adams, the celebrated photographer: "Here are worlds of experience beyond the world of aggressive man, beyond history, beyond science. The moods and qualities of nature and the relations of great art are difficult to define; we can grasp them only in the depths of our perceptive spirit."

I found such lofty expressions from statesmen, too, statesmen of both major political parties. One hundred years ago Charles Evans Hughes, Republican governor of New York and later chief justice of the Supreme Court, declared at the dedication of Palisades Interstate Park:

> Of what avail would be the benefits of gainful occupation, what would be the promise of prosperous communities, with wealth of products and freedom of exchange, were it not for opportunities to cultivate the love of

the beautiful? The preservation of the scenery of the Hudson is the highest duty with respect to this river imposed upon those who are the trustees of its manifest benefits.

In Maine, Governor Percival Baxter, the son of a wealthy family, found in Mount Katahdin the gift he wished to give with his own money to the people of Maine. By stipulating that the area "forever shall be held in its natural wild state," Governor Baxter passed on his understanding of the need for wild places in modern civilization. "The works of men are short-lived," he declared on November 30, 1941. "Monuments decay, buildings crumble and wealth vanishes, but Katahdin in its massive grandeur will forever remain the mountain of the people of Maine. Throughout the ages it will stand as an inspiration to the men and women of this State."

Attainments in preservation, as in any manifestation of ethics and idealism, do not come easily. In the case of the Wilderness Act, fruition came after eight years of discussion and debate by the Senate and House of Representatives, and after eighteen separate hearings conducted by Congressional committees around the country. I believe it would never have happened without the unflinching commitment of a very broad coalition that rallied people, all kinds of people, to the wilderness cause.

Now I believe the time is at hand to review the scope and strengths of that coalition, and to renew it to meet new challenges. On one hand, Americans can be proud of the 106 million acres safeguarded by the Wilderness Act. It defines wilderness in law and public policy, and how it should be cared for and used. It does even more, encouraging us to conserve the feeling and skills of self-reliance. That we have set aside these special places is known throughout the world; wilderness preservation treats ecology as the economics of nature, in a manner directly related to the economics of humankind. Keeping biotic diversity alive, for example, is the surest means of keeping humanity alive. But conservation transcends economics – it illuminates the human condition by refusing to put a price tag on the priceless.

On the other hand, I see the wilderness concept diluted in proposal after proposal before Congress, and in management plan after management plan prepared by our resource agencies. I feel deep concern over the impacts of overuse, misuse and commercialization; over allowing motorized equipment inside wilderness, and over the willingness to accept something-less-than-wilderness in the National Wilderness Preservation System. When you read legislation providing for "conservation, recreation and development" in the same package, you can bet your bottom dollar that wilderness protection will come last and least.

I don't mean to target any group or individuals for blame, for we are all part of the problem. More important, we can all contribute to the solution. Reconstituting the coalition – of citizen conservationists, scientists, elected public officials, public servants in the resource agencies, writers, artists and the media – will make it happen. We all love our country. Although we don't say it enough, that is what brings us together.

I think of the campaigners for the Wilderness Act as true patriots. Howard Zahniser, the principal author and advocate of the Wilderness Act of 1964, was studious, articulate and compassionate. "We are not fighting progress," Zahniser said. "We are making it. We are not dealing with a vanishing wilderness. We are working for a wilderness forever." In 1956 Representative John P. Saylor of Pennsylvania introduced the Wilderness Bill in the House of Representatives. I knew Saylor as a friend and hero. In many ways he was a conservative Republican. Nevertheless, for eight years he led the uphill legislative battle and never gave up.

I remember Senator Frank Church, of Idaho, as one of the courageous conservationists in Congress, recalling in particular the battle over reclassification of the old Idaho Primitive Area as the River of No Return Wilderness, when Senator Church conducted hearings in different sections of Idaho, and people who had never spoken publicly before stood up and responded to him, opening their hearts in praise of an area larger and wilder than Yellowstone. The designation of this great area as the Frank Church – River of No Return Wilderness certainly is a deserved recognition of Senator Church's service to his own state and the nation.

I knew and worked with able scientists, like John and Frank Craighead, the experts on the grizzly bear, and with committed wilderness advocates in the federal agencies. To my mind, Bill Worf ranks with Arthur Carhart, Robert Marshall and Aldo Leopold, Forest Service professionals who led the way in wilderness awareness and management. Worf came to Washington, DC, soon after the act was passed to write implementing regulations for the agency. He is a public servant who never quit, establishing the wonderfully constructive organization Wilderness Watch after he retired.

I've known others like him elsewhere in the Forest Service and in the other agencies as well. I think also of the late Paul Fritz. He was a feisty, stocky New Yorker, who came west to study landscape architecture at Utah

State University, worked for a time for the Forest Service, then transferred to the National Park Service. In 1966 he was placed in charge of Craters of the Moon National Monument, a striking Idaho landscape of lava fields studded with cinder cones. Disregarding bureaucratic admonitions in his own agency, he gained support from local communities and environmental groups for the Craters of the Moon wilderness, established in 1970 as the first national park unit added to the National Wilderness Preservation System.

But my favorite heroes have been my own breed, writers who were activists, like Edward Abbey, Sigurd Olson, Richard Neuberger, Wallace Stegner and Paul Brooks, and journalists, notably John Oakes, a champion of wilderness, civil rights and all good causes, who rose to be editor of the editorial page of the *New York Times*.

The best defense clearly is an aware, alert and involved public. It makes things happen. It worked in times past. It starts at the grassroots with individual citizens who care about the beauty of the earth.

Looking back, I remember environmental leaders of forty or fifty years ago as missionaries. Those people gave us broad shoulders to stand on. They want us to work together through tough and trying times, to sound the alarm and to alert the public, from the grassroots to Washington, in defense of wild places.

That is why I feel we should not allow the mismanagement of our public lands, whether in wilderness or not. I believe strongly in the principle of public land ownership and in the professional agencies that administer them. I feel alarm at moves to disassemble and privatize national parks, national forests, national wildlife refuges, and areas administered by the BLM, the Bureau of Land Management. I hope we will not allow it, for public lands are the last open spaces, last wilderness, last wildlife haven.

I feel the same about charging fees for recreation on public lands. It's a terrible idea. National parks in the United States are being reduced from sanctuaries to popcorn playgrounds, managed as theme parks in the Disney mode rather than by park professionals in the public interest.

The role of government in recreation – of government at all levels – should be to support conservation, physical fitness and healthy outdoor leisure away from a mechanized supercivilized world. A wholesome natural environment provides the foundation for a wholesome human environment. We can't have one without the other. The preservation of nature is a use in its own right – a "wise use." Gifford Pinchot, the twentieth century pioneer, said it this way:

> The planned and orderly development and conservation of our natural resources is the first duty of the United States. It is the only form of insurance that will certainly protect us against the disasters that lack of foresight has in the past repeatedly brought down on nations since passed away. A nation deprived of liberty may win it, a nation divided may reunite, but a nation whose natural resources are destroyed must inevitably pay the penalty of poverty, degradation and decay.

Perhaps the most important role of the public lands is to safeguard wilderness, nature untamed. Wilderness is at the core of a healthy society. Wilderness, above all its definitions, purposes and uses, is sacred space, with sacred power, the heart of a moral world. Wilderness preservation is not so much a system or a tactic, but a way of understanding the sacred connection with all of life, with people, plants, animals, water, sunlight, and clouds. It's an attitude and way of life with a spiritual ecological dimension.

I remember listening to Sigurd Olson speaking at the 1967 Sierra Club Biennial Wilderness Conference in San Francisco. He hadn't started as a professional writer – he had earlier been a teacher and a guide – and didn't complete his first book until he was fifty-five. Yet it became the first of nine, filled with his perceptions of North Country water wilderness in the center of the continent. Now the Sierra Club honored him with the John Muir Award for "the excellence of his writing and leadership in conservation that will truly make a difference a hundred years from now in the face of this land and in the mind of man [and woman]." This is what Sigurd said in accepting the award:

> Make the wilderness so important, so understandable, so clearly seen as vital to human happiness that it cannot be relegated to an insubstantial minority. If it affects everyone – and I believe it does – then we must find out how to tell the world why it affects everyone. Only when we put wilderness on that broad base will we have a good chance of saving it.

I thought at the time his words were a challenge meant for me. But no, they are a legacy meant for us all.

International Journal of Wilderness, 2004

Postscript: *Continuum*

I wrote earlier in this book that environmental leaders of forty or fifty years ago were missionaries who gave us broad shoulders to stand on. Yet now I recognize the world has changed dramatically since their time, and maybe mine too.

It frightens me to observe the upheaval in this country and everywhere else on earth as well. I feel strange and uncomfortable in this modern, dehumanized new age.

For example, in years past we didn't talk much about global warming because we did not fully understand it or its implications. Now I daresay that global warming is widely recognized as a threat to civilization. But it isn't simply global warming that concerns me; it's the sum and substance of its causes more than its effects.

I mean that supertechnology has led to superconsumerism, and that advanced means of production have enabled the manufacture of more goods than people need or logically can use. In consequence, to keep the system going, people must be persuaded to buy and use more, and more again, and never mind the waste of it. That is what advertising, marketing and mass media are meant to do, and why more people mean more consumers, everywhere.

In the onward march of globalized trade and commerce, every part of the world is encompassed and exploited. The earth is treated as a commodity to be surveyed, bought and sold and converted into merchandise. The air, water and land all are polluted and poisoned and degraded in the process with toxic materials applied to induce some product or other to grow faster, cheaper and more profitably.

In this global atmosphere, people are separated from land and nature. Traditions and entire cultures are overrun and obliterated. In a globalized economy, standards of living are not raised but lowered. As I see it, globalization, with its competition for materials and markets, does not bring people together as neighbors and friends but drives them apart with fear and hatred of each other. It leads to war, one war after another, in which the innocents are the victims.

While writing these lines in late 2006, I received a letter from an old friend and compadre, Dick Carter, who as director of the High Uintas Preservation Council in Utah has long labored for a noble cause "You are a true elder in the most meaningful sense of the word," he wrote," and I only wish we could step back in time where far more hope prevailed. The idea that things will always and simply get better as the arrow of time moves forward is not true."

My friend has a strong point there. History shows that yesterday's victory must be won again and again or likely will turn into tomorrow's defeat. Laws and regulations have their place, but only people make things work: people who are alert and involved and who keep in there swinging, who set their sights higher, and never lower them.

At the same time, I enjoy and find encouragement in the mood reflected in a note from Martha McCracken, a friend in Puerto Rico. She addressed the issue of global warming, but said she reminds people that even baby steps forward can make a difference. Yes, they do. Then she wrote: "If I didn't have faith I wouldn't be able to cope but I know there is a God who gives us the freedom to make a mess of our world and our lives but still loves us. I see good all around me: I see it in the laughter of children, the wisdom of the elders and the energy and hope of young people."

Personally, I wish God took a stronger hand. I've learned something about religion, though without adhering to it. I do, however, read and choose biblical selections that stir, stimulate and support ideals that reach beyond religion, such as:

"Faith is the assurance of things hoped for, the conviction of things not seen" (from Hebrews 11:1).

I cannot think of any way to say it better. But I will try to express it a little differently. Like Martha, I see good all around me, too. Earlier I said that environmental leaders of forty or fifty years ago were missionaries, and then I wrote that they want us now to work together through tough and trying times, to sound the alarm and to alert the public, from the grassroots to Washington, in defense of wild places. I know many, many people who are doing that, out of conscience and conviction, and without fear or favor. That is continuum.

Like Harvey Broome and Ernie Dickerman, the best of them get outdoors and walk the trails. That is where inspiration comes from. It doesn't come simply from reading or from office work, and certainly not from riding on a snowmobile or off-road vehicle. Those machines are the essence of superconsumerism run amok in the woods. They cause a lot of damage, to the natural resource, and to the rider as well – physically, psychologically and spiritually, giving the illusion of strength and satisfaction when the power is all in the machine and the rider's high is more like it derives from nicotine or narcotics. Fifty years ago we didn't see much of those machines and failed to realize they would prove such a nuisance. I dare to hope they will be gone in the next fifty years.

John B. Oakes was another excellent outdoors person. That is where he found his feeling for conservation as manifest in the editorial pages of the *New York Times*. In 1981 we made a dory trip together in a group down the Colorado River where it flows through the Grand Canyon. We both recognized that it takes time and patience to allow messages from the raw earth to filter through one's outer defenses and touch the inner spirit. Each day when we explored ashore, up steep canyons to springs and gardens and ancient Indian stone structures, John showed himself limber, energetic and absorbed, much as he was with the editorials of the *Times*. And that newspaper has continued, even now, to publish powerful editorials on conservation and natural resources well worthy of him. And the John B. Oakes Award for Distinguished Environmental Journalism is awarded annually by the Natural Resources Defense Council to the author of an article or series in a US newspaper or magazine that makes an exceptional contribution to public understanding of environmental issues. That is his legacy.

In this same vein, I well remember when Tom Bell founded *High Country News* and ran it as a one-man show from the back room of his home in Lander, Wyoming. Tom poured all his savings and energy into reporting western environmental issues in his fortnightly. It was hard going; ultimately Tom made certain the paper would survive and moved on. *High Country News* (or *HCN*) relocated to Paonia, in western Colorado, where it became well established and staffed, and well read and respected by people who care about the West. *HCN* has spawned many able writers who have gone out to spread the gospel. And they are Tom Bell's continuum.

A few words here about outdoor writers and writing. I was never one of them myself. For that matter, I wasn't a nature writer either. I was simply a conservation writer focused on protecting and preserving nature in the out-of-doors and in that role belonged for many years to the Outdoor

Writers Association of America (OWAA). Through good fortune, in 1994 I was awarded the Jade of Chiefs and inducted into the Circle of Chiefs, the conservation council of the OWAA, where I have connected with literate, gifted writers and conservationists, including Ted Williams, of Massachusetts, and Dan Small, of Wisconsin, who contributed the foreword and afterword to this book; Tony Dean, of South Dakota; Michael Furtman, of Minnesota; George Laycock, of Ohio; Joel Vance, of Missouri, and others as well.

For myself, I'm glad when new writers with environmental concern and commitment come along and that I can call them friends and colleagues. Here in Wisconsin Eric Hansen worked for twenty years as a machinist until he followed his heart outdoors to the hiking trails and then to writing about them. But producing two good guidebooks to the trails was not enough for Eric. In time he wrote a thoughtful, insightful essay for the *Chicago Tribune* on mining threats to special sanctuaries of the Upper Peninsula of Michigan that won an award for him. Then he published another essay, this one in the *Milwaukee Journal-Sentinel*, headlined "Behind Wisconsin Wildlife Story," and with this subhead:

A cleaner environment also benefits
The humans who watch it

Perhaps that is what it is all about. In any case, for me it's a treat when Eric comes out from Milwaukee and we walk the trails in Lion's Den County Park to the breezy overlook high above our inland ocean called Lake Michigan. It's the ideal place to share ideas and visions, and to look across the waters into forever.

Afterword

Amen, write on!

By Dan Small

Michael Frome tells it like it is. He always has, and, at the age of 86, probably always will. Most people, even muckraking environmental journalists, who have survived to that age have long since hung up their rakes and retired to a comfortable life of long naps, short walks and perhaps tending a few posies.

Not Frome.

This work is one of several he hopes yet to finish. He maintains a web site, where he regularly posts new essays; and from his Port Washington, Wisconsin, home, he sends, to a long list of correspondents, a monthly "Portogram," in which he details his most recent travels and urges the rest of us to eschew complacency and keep working for change.

In the Portogram written on the occasion of his 86th birthday, Frome asks rhetorically, "What have I accomplished? Have I done anything worthy?"

He then shares an e-mail that arrived fortuitously from a friend who cites from the concluding paragraph of a chapter Frome contributed to the 1970 book *What's Ahead for Our Public Lands*: "These lands are the treasure of the nation. Now is the crucial hour to appreciate and defend them as such."

That statement, the friend writes, is "as valid today, if not more valid than it was a generation ago!"

Frome's passion for digging out the truth on environmental and conservation issues and writing about it in clear, hard-hitting prose continues unabated. Few writers have done as much to promote natural resource conservation and the preservation of public lands.

His message today is as clear as ever, and perhaps more urgent, distilled to a keen truth that resists rebuttal. Now that he calls Wisconsin home, Frome has dived into the protection of the Great Lakes and the state's remaining open spaces.

To celebrate his 86th birthday, Frome and his wife, June Eastvold, took a boat tour through Wisconsin's great Horicon Marsh, a vast wetland that was drained, heavily exploited and virtually obliterated before being restored and protected by the Wisconsin Department of Natural Resources and the US Fish and Wildlife Service to become "one of the great birding areas of the country, if not the world." There, he witnessed the skies, lush waters and place of spring migration of thousands of water birds, "all fragments of a watery world free of commerce and human clutter, and at peace with itself."

"The lessons I learned, or relearned, from my visit," he recounts in his Portogram, "are (a) people of caring and conscience do make a difference and (b) public lands, as I wrote years ago, are the treasure of the nation. [...] Privatize the public lands? Sell them off to the highest bidder? Hell no, I say. I would rather shake up our politics with leaders and programs that really count."

Frome doesn't deny the need for development, but would like to see more of it that respects the natural landscape, with smaller homes and space for wildlife, so young people can learn about nature as earlier generations did. And he recognizes the value of strong organizations that work for conservation and the environment at the local, regional and national levels. "We're all busy with work and life today," he said. "That's why we need conservation organizations. We need coalitions to find common ground."

The Great Lakes are especially challenging because you have to take all five of them and all their tributaries into comprehensive programming." He believes the fishermen, boaters and others must see the bigger picture and form coalitions in order to save the lakes from perils such as the invasion of exotic species and increasing demand for water from outside the watershed.

Frome writes almost daily in his home office, often at a pace that would exhaust a younger man. He is currently writing his autobiography, and he is a speaker at national and international conferences. Asked why he's still an activist at an age when most people are content to watch TV or play cards, Frome said, "Because there's so much to be done and damn few who are doing it. Somebody's got to tell it like it is."

A birthday card he received included a passage from Thoreau that aptly describes Frome, the passionate environmentalist, tireless crusader, hell-raising octogenarian:

> A gentle rain makes the grass many shades greener. So our prospects

brighten on the influx of better thoughts. We should be blessed if we lived in the present always, and took advantage of every accident that befell us, like the grass which confesses the influence of the slightest dew that falls on it; and did not spend our time in atoning for the neglect of past opportunities, which we call doing our duty. We loiter in winter while it is already spring.

This message from an equally passionate environmental activist reminds Frome that he does not want to loiter in winter, atoning for neglect of past opportunities: "I want to make the most of life, without worry of how much is left of it, and to share the best of it with loved ones and friends..."

Amen, Mike. Write on!

Wisconsin Outdoor News, 2004, updated 2006

Index

Michael Frome is well known as author, educator and tireless champion of America's natural heritage. Born in New York City, Michael served as a World War II navigator, flying to distant corners of the world. He began his writing career as a newspaper reporter for the *Washington Post* and later served as a successful travel writer before concentrating on the environment and the out-of-doors.

Over the years he has been a featured columnist in *Field & Stream, Los Angeles Times, American Forests* and *Defenders of Wildlife* and has written eighteen books. After years as a journalist, he began a new career in higher education, teaching at the universities of Idaho and Vermont, Northland College and Western Washington University.

He earned a doctorate in 1993 from the Union Institute (which in 1999 named him Outstanding Alumnus of the Year). He retired in 1995 from the faculty of Western Washington University, at Bellingham, Washington, where he directed a pioneering program in environmental journalism and writing. The University of Idaho established in his honor the Michael Frome Scholarship for Excellence in Conservation Writing.

He now lives at Port Washington, Wisconsin, with his wife, June Eastvold, a poet and retired Lutheran pastor.

* * * * * * * *

Ted Williams has written eloquently about fishing, the environment and outdoors ethics for *Audubon, Fly Rod & Reel* and other publications. He is author of *The Insightful Sportsman* and *Wild Moments*.

Dan Small has been host/producer of Outdoor Wisconsin on public television since it began twenty-plus years ago. He co-hosts a weekly radio show and is contributing editor of *Wisconsin Outdoor News*.